Change Your Life

Books by Becky Tirabassi

change your life Daily Journal

change your life Daily Bible

How to Live with Them
Since You Can't Live Without Them

Let Faith Change Your Life

Let Prayer Change Your Life

Let Prayer Change Your Life Workbook

Thoroughly Fit Devotional

My Partner Prayer Notebook

Most Berkley Books are available at special quantity discounts for bulk purchases for sales promotions, premiums, fund-raising, or educational use. Special books, or book excerpts, can also be created to fit specific needs.

For details, write: Special Markets, The Berkley Publishing Group, 375 Hudson Street, New York, New York 10014.

Change Your Life

ACHIEVE A HEALTHY BODY,

HEAL RELATIONSHIPS

& CONNECT WITH GOD

Becky Tirabassi

BERKLEY BOOKS, NEW YORK

A Berkley Book
Published by The Berkley Publishing Group
A division of Penguin Putnam Inc.
375 Hudson Street
New York, New York 10014

Copyright © 1999 by Becky Tirabassi
Cover design by Lisa Amoroso
Photograph of the author copyright © 1999 by Russ Harrington
Text design by Jennifer Ann Daddio

Scripture taken from the Holy Bible, New International Version R. Copyright © 1973, 1978, 1984 by International Bible Society. Used by permission of Zondervan Publishing House. All rights reserved.
"Food Guide Pyramid" and "How to Use the Daily Food Chart" reprinted with permission of the Cooper Institute.
The NIV and New International Version trademarks are registered in the United States Patent and Trademark Office by International Bible Society. Use of either trademark requires the permission of International Bible Society.
Scripture quotations marked (NLT) are taken from the Holy Bible, New Living Translation. Copyright © 1996. Used by permission of Tyndale House Publishers Inc., Wheaton, Illinois 60189. All rights reserved.

PRINTING HISTORY
G. P. Putnam's Sons hardcover edition / December 1999
Berkley trade paperback edition / January 2001

Berkley trade paperback ISBN: 0-425-17819-6

The Penguin Putnam Inc. World Wide Web site address is
http://www.penguinputnam.com

The Library of Congress has catalogued the G. P. Putnam's Sons hardcover edition as follows:

Tirabassi, Becky, date.
Change your life : achieve a healthy body, heal relationships, and connect with God / by Becky Tirabassi.
p. cm.
ISBN 0-399-14543-5
1. Success. 2. Change (Psychology). 3. Change—Religious aspects.
I. Title.
BJ1611.T57 2000 99-049931 CIP
158—dc21

PRINTED IN THE UNITED STATES OF AMERICA

10 9 8 7 6 5 4 3 2 1

Acknowledgments

I have spent many years on the journey to change my life. Many people have loved and forgiven me, believed in me and graciously helped me change, heal, and balance my life.

I want to personally thank each of you for keeping me accountable to sustain many positive and powerful changes in my life.

Mom and Dad—Thank you for never giving up on me.

Ralph—Thank you for looking beyond who I was and showing me the way to God.

Roger—I can't imagine my life without you.

Jake—Your life has given me my best material!

Mrs. Bette Nichols—You were my first mentor. I will never forget you.

Claudia Cross—Thank you for believing in me and the **change your life** message.

Denise Silvestro—You were meant to be my editor—I knew it! Your editorial gift has given me the ability to turn this message into a book! This is a dream come true.

The "CYL" Staff:

Heidi Sisto—I am so fortunate that God sent you to me to run our office!

Heather Vodra—Your poise, expertise, and fun personality are terrific!

Carissa Dunn—Thank you for being such a loyal friend and coworker.

Jean Hunter—Your meticulous, consistent work in the office is greatly appreciated.

Jennifer Hansen—Thank you for your incredible ability to type manuscripts and format radio shows.

Lynn Bender—Your tireless, efficient commitment to CYL inspires all of us.

Lisa Morsey—Your confidence, counsel, and expertise are great support to me!

Jill Heatherly—Thank you for your editorial "eye" and willingness to help me with the Leader's Guide!

My "CYL" Group:

Jennifer, Lynn, Lisa, and Jill of my staff—Thank you for the double duty. Cindy Christeson—Your friendship is a great source of strength to me.

Stephanie Watring—I'm so proud that you have pursued the dream in your heart.

Kathy Theide—Thank you for being a good sport, neighbor!

Joe Battaglia—Thank you for your guidance and help in producing the "Change your life Daily" radio shows!

Judy Hilsinger—Your belief and confidence in the **change your life** message has been a great source of support to me.

Julie Walker, Rae Smith, and Michelle Whitworth—Thank you for the special touches each of you adds to my life.

Ron and Alexa Jensen—Your friendship continually encourages me to grow spiritually, mentally, emotionally, and physically!

Kyle Webb—I greatly appreciate your willingness, patience,

and diligence to turn the **change your life** concept into powerful resources to share with others.

Prayer Team Members—Each month your prayers have empowered and sustained us at **change your life!**

Steve Arterburn—Thank you for the many, many years of support you have given to me, and to my company.

The WOF Team—Thank you for the way that you allow me to dream big dreams by sharing this message with thousands!!

Mark Taylor—Thank you for partnering with me on **The change your life Daily Journal** and **The change your life Daily Bible!!** Your commitment and integrity in the process have been wonderful.

To every sojourner
on the quest to change your life.
Be encouraged,
Becky

Contents

Change Your Life

Life Is All About Change

Over the past fifteen years, I have had the wonderful and exciting opportunity to travel throughout the United States, encouraging and motivating tens of thousands of men, women, and students each year to change their lives.

In airplanes, week after week, I sit next to the CEOs of nationally known companies, entertainment lawyers, salesmen and saleswomen, chefs, television personalities, and politicians. At events, I speak to teenage, single, married, divorced, successful, broken, and powerful people. I haven't found a person yet who doesn't want to change one or many areas of their lives.

The Sit-Down Game

At my **change your life** events, I play the Sit-Down Game, an "ice breaker" from my youth-worker days. Everyone loves a fun game, so I am greeted by hundreds of smiling, eager faces. Starting them all out on a level playing field, I ask everyone to stand up. With everyone in the room on their feet, I tell them that I am going to make a series of statements. If their answer is "yes" to any of the statements, that is their cue to sit down. When they are already seated, and I make a statement or ask a question that applies to them, then they should raise one finger for each additional time their answer is "yes."

Imagine, right now, that you are in a roomful of strangers and are asked to stand.

I say, "Sit down if you are currently mad at your mother."

Everyone hesitates, and looks around the room. This statement is a tough question to answer quickly. Most people don't really want to admit—in public—that they are at odds with their mother. Slowly, a handful of people shrug their shoulders, and sit down.

My next statement is, "Sit down if you have agonized over a teenager in the past week." Almost half the room noisily sits down or raises a finger. They are admitting that emotional or verbal struggles with their teenager have occurred in their home recently. (Parents of teenagers know that a week without experiencing even a little tension with the kids is a rarity.) I jokingly add, "I see that only single people and parents of toddlers are left standing in the room!"

Just so no one feels left out, I make another, similar statement, "Sit down or raise a finger if you have yelled at a child this week." By now, every parent in the room is sitting.

I am on a roll now! Few attendees are still standing, or seated without two or three fingers raised. Knowing that everyone in the room has become more vulnerable (and maybe even a little more honest), I say, "How many of you have you been trying unsuccessfully to lose five . . . (I pause for a few seconds . . .) or fifty pounds?" Their response is predictable. First, the whole room laughs uproariously. Then, almost everyone left standing drops into a seat, vividly expressing their frustration. Those who are already seated begin to wave their whole hand at me! We laugh together. Of course, this is an unofficial poll, but it seems as if almost every person in the room has been trying to lose weight or inches, find time in their schedules to work out, and has been wondering how to balance this area with every other area of their lives.

By this time, we are all feeling much more comfortable with each other. But I still need just a few more illustrations to prove my point. You see, I am convinced that every single person who has come to a **change your life** event has been struggling with how to make changes in their lives either physically, emotionally, spiritually, or mentally. This little game helps those who are completely unaware—or have been in denial—become more aware that certain areas of their lives need to change. Many attending the event *know* they need to change, and have made many attempts to change, but have not found a practical, life-long strategy for change. Others might be so overwhelmed by the many areas of their lives that are out of control that they don't know where to begin to make changes that will last. What has become most evident is that everyone who has come to the **change your life** event has one or more areas of their lives that need to change.

We keep playing.

Next, I say, "Sit down or raise a finger if there is someone in your life you are currently struggling to forgive." Now I have hit a chord. The laughter has ceased, but the hearts have become soft and vulnerable. Most of us have learned how to pretend in front of others that our relationships are healthy when they are not. We avoid, deny, or hide the heartache.

As people slowly sit or hesitantly raise a finger, they silently acknowledge that people whom they love have hurt them, and they have hurt people whom they love. Without words, they admit that they are at an impasse in one or more relationships.

Within five minutes of the start of the event, I have exposed everyone in the room to each other's weaknesses, and it is apparent that we all share similar struggles. We share a common desire to change, but few of us are up for the hard work, long haul, or difficult road ahead. Instead, most of us have become complacent, give up, procrastinate, rationalize, or simply set our dreams aside because change is "too hard," "will take too much effort," or "appears impossible."

There is one more question that I am confident will seat the final few stragglers. I ask, "How many of you have a dream in your heart that won't go away?"

Every face in the room has a wistful expression. We don't have to be the same age or gender or marital status to have a dream. I have found a common chord once again.

Then comes the redeeming moment. I ask anyone to **stand up** if they would like to make changes in their life . . .

physically,
mentally,
emotionally, or
spiritually.

The room is full of hundreds of people standing—even jumping—up cheering and applauding themselves. I am now looking at a crowd that is no longer reluctant to admit they need to change. Their response tells me that they are ready, hopeful, and excited to change. Their enthusiasm tells me that this audience expects to be encouraged and inspired to change their lives.

Perhaps I am compelled by an inward driving force to encourage those whose lives have spun out of control because *I* have struggled in so many areas of my life—and yet found help and motivation to change my life for the better!

In my forty-four years of life, I have struggled with . . .

alcoholism,
overeating,
exercising obsessively—or not at all,
outbursts of anger (especially at my child),
unforgiveness toward my mother,
resentment for being rejected,
sexual immorality,
envy toward those who were skinnier, richer, or prettier than I,
procrastination, and even
prayerlessness—

each of which has had paralyzing effects on me and my relationship with God and others.

I have discovered—firsthand—that it is not only the destitute, spiritually lost, or morally impure who struggle with conflict, addiction, and weakness. Every human being struggles. We might not talk about our problems. We might not even want to admit them to ourselves. But they do exist. And if these destructive weaknesses find a home in our heart, mind, or body, they will take over and steal everything—from our daily happiness to our purpose for living!

But I have also experienced that no matter how lost you are, how far you have strayed, or how broken you have become, you can change your life for the better, *beginning today*. I am convinced that there is no struggle too great to overcome. I do not believe that there is a problem too complicated to solve, an issue too large to tackle, or a relationship too damaged to mend.

Why am I so confident? I have proof. I have lived it.

I have overcome alcoholism and drug addiction, and recently celebrated my twenty-second year of sobriety.

I have experienced an incredible amount of healing in my once very stormy relationship with my mother.

I have a great, fun relationship with my twenty-year-old son.

I have maintained the same weight for over ten years, after having yo-yoed up and down the scale from my teens into my thirties. In addition, I have worked out three (not five, six, or seven) times a week for over fifteen years, when I previously could not maintain a consistent workout program.

I have a great peace and purpose in my life that I attribute to the habit of connecting with God through journaling for one hour each day for the past fifteen years.

I have been faithfully and happily married for twenty-two years.

My father was a factory worker and an alcoholic who was raised by an alcoholic. He was never able to financially provide for me to go to college or receive any inheritance. These facts have not kept me from starting my own business and owning my own company for over fifteen years. The success of this **change your life** message has allowed me to maintain a small staff for ten years and to give away three times more money each year than I ever made working for another company.

Finally, I am considered by many to be a disciplined, organized, prompt, reliable person. This is a complete turnaround from the time in my life when I was completely undisciplined, disorganized, always late, and unreliable.

Need I say more?

I have found the key to changing your life.

This book is not a theory. The **change your life** balanced philosophy is not simply a good idea. It is a proven, practical plan to change your life.

As you begin to read through the pages of this book, you will be asked questions that have a purpose. If you have been unaware or unwilling to discover the areas of your life that are out of control or that need change, these questions will expose the truth about yourself—to yourself.

If you are stuck in unhealthy relationships, a mediocre job, a poor financial position, or you repeat harmful or self-destructive behavior, it is time to change. But in order to change you must first acknowledge the reality of your weight problem, relationship problems, spiritual void, or tendency to fall into workaholic or lazy lifestyles. In the privacy of this book, you can become aware of those areas that need to change.

Next, you will be challenged to admit to yourself, others, and God that you *want* to change. This may sound very difficult. Yet, I believe that your reluctance to admit to others that you have a problem could be the very thing that is stopping you from healing, moving forward, excelling, producing your best effort, or even finding your life mate. Holding on to secrets, pride, and yes, sin, holds you back from change.

Trust me on this.

Power is released when you publicly admit your shortcomings. Millions have experienced this phenomenon in church meetings and in programs such as Alcoholics Anonymous. But you don't have to be an alcoholic to admit that you need to change certain areas of your life. Anyone will benefit from the healing that comes from admission or confession. Admission is crucial to change. This second step will be the hardest, but I will encourage you along the way with stories and examples of those who have been empowered to change through transparent honesty with themselves, God, and others.

Next, I promise to motivate each of you to achieve your desired changes through a practical action plan.

Imperative to your success will be your willingness to make a journal appointment with yourself—and God—for thirty minutes each day. **The change your life Daily Journal** is the sixty-day spiral notebook that I have designed—and tens of thousands use—to record desired changes and chart progress of 8 Daily To Do's on four journal pages:

Physical: Eat right and Exercise regularly
Emotional: Forgive and Give
Spiritual: Talk to God and Listen to God
Mental: Detail Your Day and Define Your Dream

Whether you use **The change your life Daily Journal** (see order form in back of book) or create your own journal using a three-ringed binder or a spiral notebook, through the daily practice of journaling you will see change in your life as a result of turning your good intentions into a practical, daily action plan.

Finally, I contend—and have found—that the key to sustaining change in your life comes as a result of being accountable to others. When you know that people are supporting and encouraging you, you remain responsible and committed to the changes you are trying to make.

Believing strongly that everyone should have an accountability group of their own, I will give you suggestions and guidelines, as well as examples from my own life, on how to start a **change your life Group** in your home or office.

You *can* change your life beginning today. I'm here to help you.

ONE

Change Begins with Awareness

Everyone I have ever met has struggled with or knows someone who struggles with . . .

an addiction,
an eating disorder,
a disappointment that won't fade away,
a habit that they can't seem to overcome,
an unwillingness or an inability to forgive those who might
    have hurt them,
a deep spiritual void that they are uncertain how to fill, or
feelings of helplessness and hopelessness.

Most likely, you have picked up this book because you have become aware of one area—or many areas—of *your* life that needs to change.

Perhaps . . .

- your clothes don't fit the same as last year?
- your close friend or coworker is irritated with you?
- you lack peace and simmer with impatience?

- you are more often dissatisfied with your life than content with it?
- you are frustrated with your lack of discipline to exercise, save money, or be on time?
- you hunger for spiritual knowledge and growth but do nothing to attain it?
- you struggle with debt?
- you have a hidden secret or addiction that you've told no one about?

You are not alone.

Perhaps you, like I, have believed that *if only* you had a quick fix, an effortless solution would solve your problems and give you the momentum, money, or magic to change your life.

Experience, more than any other expert, has proven that to achieve and sustain long-lasting change in any area of your life—whether physically, emotionally, spiritually, or mentally—you need time, discipline, and a regular commitment.

Weight lifters, runners, teachers, and investors will tell you that if you apply discipline to an area of your life, and it is sustained over time, it possesses incredible power to change your life. But if discipline is ignored, it possesses an equal amount of power to hinder or even halt your progress to positively change your life. True change occurs because a series of events and actions accumulates *over time* to achieve a new result. Herein lies the challenge to change. Change is difficult, it takes time, and doesn't usually happen overnight. So, where and how can you find the courage and access the power to change?

I believe that you can change your life beginning today. Through this book, I'd like inspire you to look at change as manageable, possible, and achievable, rather than difficult, impossible, or unreachable. It is my goal to encourage you to consider change as a four-step process that begins with *awareness,* is empowered by *admission,* achieved through a *daily action plan,* and sustained with *accountability.*

A Rude Awakening . . .

My journey to change began with an awareness that I am—and always will be—an alcoholic. A beer-drinking, disco-dancing, smart-mouthed teenager growing up in Cleveland, Ohio, I graduated from high school at seventeen, moved away from home, enrolled into and dropped out of college by 1974, and moved to California before my nineteenth birthday.

It was a time when youth expressed itself in everything from the dreaminess of becoming a beach boy or beach bunny, to the search for psychedelic happiness in the hippie movement. In the '70s, America's youth took the initiative to freely experiment with, explore, and embrace sex, drugs, and alcohol.

Although I was raised in a conservative midwestern town, I had an adventurous, curious, almost wild side to me. At the age of nineteen, without much reservation, I drove straight to the West Coast and flung myself into drugs, dope, nightclub dancing, binge drinking, and living with boyfriends.

By twenty-one, I had fallen to a point of personal destruction, but I was still unaware of how out of control my life had become.

When I returned to Ohio to be in a girlfriend's wedding, however, I proceeded to smoke and drink to excess on the night of the bachelorette party. The next morning, I woke up in bed next to a man I barely knew. I was humiliated that I had no recollection of what I had done with him the night before.

My first thought was, "Becky, do you know what they call

girls like this?" My second thought was, "You would never have done this if you hadn't been drinking."

I asked him for a ride home, walked into my mother's front door, and said, "Mom, I think I'm an alcoholic." That day, I *knew* I had more than a drinking problem. I didn't need to read a book, fill out a questionnaire, attend a meeting, or take a physical exam to prove that alcohol controlled my life.

I was familiar with alcoholism. I was the child, grandchild, and niece of men and women whose lives were controlled by alcohol. I had seen live demonstrations of how alcohol could squeeze and steal life, money, and dreams from individuals and families.

But I had never seen an alcoholic who had fully quit drinking and enjoyed a successful life. And like many people my age, I had the impression that alcoholism affected only forty- and fifty-year-olds, not athletic, fun-loving, twenty-one-year-olds.

Upon returning to California, I had every intention to quit drinking, but I planned to do it without changing my friends or lifestyle. That effort lasted only a few days—or perhaps it was hours—before I began to go through withdrawal and anxiety attacks, desperate to have a drink.

Without actually saying the words, "I'm an alcoholic," I tried to subtly tell my friends that I thought I had a serious drinking problem. Their advice to me was to "just slow down." They didn't want to believe that I had a problem. They didn't want me to change. They didn't want me to stop buying drugs or having those great parties! They were in as much denial as I wanted to be.

Talking to my friends about my problem didn't make my addiction go away. Reluctantly, I decided to go—by myself—to a traditional meeting for alcoholics. I was hoping to find a quick solution to a long-standing problem. When an older man met me at the door of the coffee-smelling, smoke-filled room and said, "Hi. I'm Joe. I've been an alcoholic for twenty years," I knew I would never return. I vividly remember thinking, "Joe, I'm not coming here for twenty years to get better—*with you!*" I could not accept that my problem was going to be a lifelong battle. I wanted help *now.*

I sunk deeper into despair, wondering how to rid myself of the compulsion to have a drink. I became extremely fearful that if I had even one drink, I could lose control and black out, pass out, or worse—end up in bed with someone else I didn't know! I grew more emotionally and physically unstable with each passing day.

Only three weeks had passed since the wedding incident when I had to appear at a court hearing for a car accident I had been in one year earlier—while drinking. On the way to the court hearing, I became paranoid that my once harmless, fun lifestyle of drinking, smoking, and partying was turning into a horrible legal ordeal.

I was emotionally broken, physically addicted, spiritually bankrupt, and mentally losing sight of reality. It was as if—all at once—I became strangely and painfully aware of who I had become; how I existed on substances, rather than food; how poorly I treated people; how deceitful I was; and how far my body and appearance had declined. I could no longer deny the sad and shameful reality of my life, nor did I want to live any longer.

Before I walked into the court building, I determined that *everything* about my life must change. I just had no idea where to begin.

Prior to the deposition, my lawyer firmly grabbed my elbow and whispered, "Rebecca, if you lie on the stand, you will be crucified." Can you remember an event, a song, or a sentence that stopped you dead in your tracks, rerouted your life, and sent you reeling in another direction? That sentence got my attention. More specifically, that was the sentence when *God* got my attention.

Alhough I felt fearful and hopeless, something deep in my soul was telling me that I needed something or Someone to take control of my life. I could no longer cover up, lie about, deny, or rationalize my state of being. I was completely aware of—and personally sick of—my addictive, deceitful life. I was determined never to live another day in such a depraved state.

The lawyer's words echoed over and over in my mind. I began to think that God was trying to reach out to me. Through the visual picture of crucifixion, I was reminded of the stories I had heard in church as a child. As a family, we had attended church every week. I knew all about God, but not since I was a little girl had I thought about being in a relationship with Him.

If I had been running from God, it was in that courtroom that I realized I was now desperately searching for a way to connect with Him. That day I was aware that I wanted to run into His arms and be held by Him like a lost child returning safely home.

My mind raced with thoughts of how I might do that. I felt drawn to God. I sensed that He truly loved me, wanted to help me, and was willing to forgive me. Oddly, I didn't feel unworthy or afraid or ashamed. I was beginning to feel hopeful.

It was the thought of a living, loving God that compelled me to get into my car and drive to a church right after the hearing. Although I didn't even know the name of the church that I drove to, or the name of its pastor, I pulled into the parking lot, fully expecting to find God. I ran frantically and tearfully down a flight of steps. I desperately knew that every area of my life needed to change.

Oddly, I didn't find the pastor. Rather, it was the janitor of the church, Ralph, who found me crying in the basement hallway. He listened to me pour out the sordid details of my broken life. Ralph told me that he, too, had been addicted. He could tell that

I was about to self-destruct from the torment of anxiety attacks, suicidal thoughts, and withdrawals that were common to an addict.

This stranger, whose last name I can't even remember, led me to God.

Through a simple, but incredibly transparent and powerful prayer with the janitor of the church, I found God waiting for me. By pouring out the sordid details of my past and present, I received a spiritual cleansing, like a shower of healing and renewal for my mind, body, and spirit. That encounter with God on August 26, 1976, was only the beginning of my lifelong journey to change every area of my life.

Within minutes I had an entirely new perspective about my life! Up until that moment, I had been completely blind to my self-destruction, but now I could plainly see the power that drugs and alcohol had over me, how they were hurting, even destroying, me. The lies that I had believed, such as "I am more fun when I drink" or "if I live with my boyfriend he will marry me," were exposed. I suddenly understood that my barriers to sobriety and wholeness were not just my physical and psychological addictions to the drugs and alcohol but the very places I chose to hang out and the various people with whom I would drink, party, or buy drugs from. It was a rude awakening to see so clearly the truth about myself, but it was an essential first step to finding the path to begin a new life.

Change—in any aspect of life—begins with awareness, and I am confident that you can begin the process of change *today* if you will:

1. Identify the truth about yourself
2. Expose the lies that you have believed

3. Name the barriers that keep you from change, and
4. List the benefits of leaving those lies and barriers behind!

Identify the Truth

It is probably no secret to you—or others—that one or more areas of your life need to change for the better. A harmless way to begin the identification process is to ask specific questions of yourself and answer them honestly:

- Has someone you love or respect made you aware of the problem?
- Have you disappointed someone or yourself because of this behavior?
- Have you physically or emotionally hurt yourself or another because of this problem?
- Have you covered up or lied about this problem?
- Have you lost something significant because of this problem (savings, relationships, possessions, self-esteem)?

In the awareness step of change, you must accept who you are, where you've been, what your patterns are, and acknowledge what you have to work with. Life becomes much more manageable when you understand that you are a unique individual with certain inherited weaknesses and strengths that will forever be a part of your life. For example, I will always be an alcoholic, therefore I can never have a drink. Because I know this about myself, I can never enjoy a champagne toast at a wedding or have a relaxing glass of wine before dinner.

I have other persistent traits. For instance, I have the tendency to burst out in anger. Because I am aware of this, I have made it a habit to journal on a daily basis about unresolved issues or anger I am experiencing. I also am committed to quickly making amends with people whom I might have hurt with my anger. And I have asked a small group of friends to keep me accountable to a lifestyle of controlling my emotions.

I can also be fiercely competitive. This can quickly escalate into envy if I am not acutely aware of the thoughts that can trip me up in this area. In addition to journaling about current situations that can cause me to be envious, I am also a part of an accountability group where I am continually transparent and vulnerable with this struggle.

Fortunately, becoming aware of one area of your life that needs to change often leads to an awareness of other areas of your life that are also out of balance. Often you become aware of problems in your life because of financial difficulties, a struggling marriage, or professional instability. You might have dug yourself into a hole of debt, been unfaithful to a marriage partner, or lied to your coworkers to hide an addiction. These problems have the potential to add more chaos and stress to your life, causing you to avoid making a move toward changing *any* area of your life.

It is important to accept that your problems will not easily—or magically—disappear. You should consider it an unrealistic expectation to dream that they will. They *might* have an apparently quick resolution, but to truly achieve long-lasting change, you will have to enter into a process that includes the help of others. For hope, healing, and health to be fully restored in your life, you must start the process of change that begins with awareness. As you become aware of the truth about yourself and your situation, and persevere through the following steps of admission, an action plan, and accountability, your life will change for the better.

Expose the Lies

To help you identify and accept the reality of your situation, it is necessary to expose the lies that you have believed—and perhaps even cherished—about this problem, issue, or harmful relationship. Why? Because the lies have kept you from making desired changes in your life!

Many of us never even attempt to change a negative aspect of our lives, reach our goals, overcome our past, or attain self-control because we "buy into" paralyzing thoughts, such as:

- "I can't do it."
- "I'm not good enough."
- "It will never happen."
- "It will cause too much pain."
- "I'm not strong enough."
- "I'll lose everything."

The reasons we all allow these negative thoughts to have so much power range from defensive, protective behavior to a stubborn or lazy aspect of our personality. The truth is that we all entertain these thoughts to a certain degree. How quickly we release them from our hearts and minds will determine how quickly we can move away from our problems and addictions to pursue new, more healthy ways of thinking and living.

As you expose the lies that you have cultivated, you first will have to identify them and then replace them with new thoughts. In the process, you also will become aware of repeated excuses you use or a habit of blaming others rather than taking responsibility for your actions. If you fail to recognize and intentionally eliminate these destructive patterns, they will continue to keep you from making desired changes in your life.

Some common lies are:

- "This is not my fault, it is _____'s fault."
- "I'm too old to change."
- "I'm not rich enough, smart enough, pretty enough, or powerful enough."
- "I can't forgive them."
- "I'm too tired."
- "It will take too much money to do this."

Journaling has been one of the most practical ways I have found to expose the negative thoughts that creep into my mind. Not only does journaling take my emotional temperature (feelings of sadness, or fear, or anxiety), but if I articulate in writing any of the thoughts that I consider to be "lies," I am immediately more aware that I need to revert to more positive thoughts, such as:

- What part of this problem is my fault? Is there anything I need to do or say to be part of solving this problem?
- I am obviously struggling with changing a specific action. Who, what, or which organization (e.g., a counselor, a smoking patch, or Weight Watchers) could offer me consultation or advice on how to find a solution to this long-standing problem?

- I refuse to focus on what I don't have. Today, I will make a list of the many, many aspects of my life that are good, positive, and strong. I will focus on those attributes and use them more effectively to change this situation.

- I am struggling to forgive someone. This means that I have to dig a little deeper into my heart, mind, and spirit and look at this situation from a different perspective. I might need to seek out a more spiritual approach to forgiveness, rather than an intellectual or emotional approach.

- I am regularly fatigued. Does my tiredness reflect a lack of exercise or poor eating habits? Am I staying up too late? Do I have enough recreation in my life? Am I overcommitted? Do I need to eliminate anything from my schedule? Should I see a doctor? Should I join a gym?

- Perhaps I don't have the money right now to fulfill this dream, but what can I do to raise the money, or how long will it realistically take to save money I need? (Robert Schuller's quote has always inspired me: "You don't have a money problem, you have an idea problem.")

What are some of the lies that you have believed?

_____

_____

_____

_____

What are some new thoughts that you could entertain?

_____

_____

_____

_____

Name the Barriers

There are also significant barriers that will keep you from seeing the areas in your life that need to change. They come in the form of negative feelings, economic or environmental circumstances, lazy habits, or excuses. They work against you. They are powerful enough to keep you from succeeding.

In order to break through the barriers, you must first identify the thoughts, feelings, habits, and excuses that keep you from achieving a healthy body, improving your relationships, or connecting with God.

The following questions are designed to help you become aware of barriers that may be holding you back from changing one or more areas in your life. Answer them honestly. No one is looking or listening . . . yet.

Identifying Barriers

PHYSICAL

- Do you come from or live near an ethnic or cultural area that provides certain unhealthy foods for the main courses, snacks, desserts, etc.?
- Do you plan your meals ahead of time in order to have the right foods for you at mealtime? (Example: Do you pack your lunch? Or eat whatever is quick or given to you? If you travel, do you order special meals ahead of time or bring healthy snacks so that you are not tempted?)
- Do you tend to pick up a few pounds each winter due to more time spent indoors than outdoors?

- Do you wear loose-fitting clothes so that you can eat more and still be comfortable?
- Do clothes from one year or six months ago still fit you?
- Do you feel sluggish, tired, or lethargic after a meal?
- Do you eat everything on your plate, even though you are full?
- Has a doctor told you that you need to lose weight and lower your cholesterol? Have you followed his/her advice?
- Are you frustrated with how you look and feel and with how much you weigh?
- Do you often find yourself buying junk food from a vending machine?
- Were you recently embarrassed to go someplace or see someone because you had gained weight?
- Do you eat standing up or quickly?
- Has someone (friend, relative, or stranger) said something that hurt your feelings regarding your weight or size?
- Do you miss physical activity, but simply cannot make time for it? Or do you really dislike or are too tired for exercise?
- Are you tempted to join a club or buy a piece of workout equipment, but do not want to spend the money?
- Do you make excuses for your weight gain, rather than owning up to overeating or lack of exercise?
- Do you tell people your true weight or your "hoped-for" weight?
- Can you name one or two major events or reasons that exercise has been crowded out of your schedule?

Answering specific questions about your eating and exercise habits will help identify the specific behaviors that prevent you from improving. If you find yourself eating candy or snacks, then this is an indication that you are hungry (or bored) and would benefit from planning low-calorie, healthy snacks. If you resist working out alone, enlist the power of a partner to keep you accountable. If you can't fit into your clothes from one year ago, acknowledge that you need to increase your activity level and reduce your fat and calorie intake with a practical, manageable plan.

Acknowledge the amount of weight you have gained and accept that, if it didn't appear overnight, it won't disappear overnight. A daily approach to eating right and exercising regularly will produce results—over time!

EMOTIONAL

- Do you hold on to memories of instances when you have been hurt, betrayed, or slighted?
- Do you become easily angered by your spouse or children (or even pets), when the very same situation with a coworker or acquaintance would incur much less reaction from you? Why do you think this is so?
- Did you go to bed with unresolved anger toward anyone lately?
- Do you gossip (or speak unkindly) about people?
- Do you purposely withhold helpful information from another because it might be used to surpass you?
- Do you desire more intimate and meaningful relationships but find them hard to hold on to?
- Do you often regret what you said to someone, especially because it was harsh?
- Do you usually find everyone but yourself at fault?
- Do you make it a habit to ask yourself where you are at fault in a disagreement?
- Are you aware of anyone who won't speak to you?
- Are you generally generous, or reluctant to give?

- Are you ever called "selfish" by those closest to you?
- Have you ever or do you currently volunteer your time for a nonprofit organization or church?
- Do you choose the best slice or give it to another?
- Do you admire those who give abundantly and with abandon, or do you consider them foolish?
- Do you look for opportunities to give?
- Do you find it harder to give of your time, money, or possessions? (Any insights into why?)
- Do you complain about something but are not willing to pitch in to help improve it?

If you have answered many of the Emotional questions with answers that reflect great anxiety, helplessness, hopelessness, or anger, this will indicate that there are issues and relationships in your life that need healing. The Bible speaks of love, joy, peace, patience, kindness, gentleness, faithfulness, and self-control as *healthy* feelings, thoughts, and reactions. When you have emotional responses and actions opposite to those named above, this can be an indication that you have room for emotional improvement.

Again, I have found that a purposeful, daily journal experience allows me to identify the barriers that undermine my emotional health. It is also the place where I am more open to becoming forgiving, understanding, apologetic, and determined to exhibit self-control in the future.

SPIRITUAL

- Have you ever been disappointed by God? (Explain.)
- What is the reason you are in a relationship with God? (If you are unsure of how to be in a relationship with God, explain.)

- Have you wanted to develop your spirituality but don't really know where to start?
- Are you currently searching for God? (Explain.)
- If you could speak to God about anything—right now—what would it be?
- What methods have you tried before or are currently using to connect with God?
- Do you expect God to answer you when you talk to Him?
- Are you familiar with the Bible? Briefly explain your knowledge of it.
- Do you get discouraged not knowing if God hears you?
- Are you doing something that you don't think God would want you to do?
- If you are running from having a relationship with God, why? Is spiritual growth important to you? (Explain.)
- Are you looking for answers about life after death?
- Do you believe that your life has a purpose? Have you discovered your purpose for life on this earth?
- Have you ever written down your prayers or conversations with God?
- Are you disillusioned by any childhood experiences regarding the God of the Bible?
- Do you feel that there is a significant piece (and peace) missing in your life that is never filled by external or material possessions or success?
- Do you have any fear of dying?
- Is there any shame or guilt in your life that you repeatedly think about?

The barriers that arise in this area of your life might be a result of a childhood misconception about God or because of a negative experience you have had with a specific religion. The purpose of the above questions is to encourage you to focus on your spirituality and having a relationship with God, rather than focusing on a particular religion. Your answers will help you identify any barriers in your life that have kept you from developing a personal relationship with the living, loving God.

MENTAL

- Do you usually leave things for the last minute?
- Do you feel like you're always "under the gun," always rushing?
- Do you almost never, often, or almost always pay your bills on time?
- Are you almost never, often, or almost always late for meetings, dates, appointments, etc.?
- Do you owe over $50 in finance charges at this time?
- Do you have any debt outside of car or mortgage payments?
- Do you live paycheck to paycheck?
- Do you use more than one calendar at this time? (Explain.)
- Do you make lists?
- Do you prioritize your lists?
- Do you check off completed tasks on your lists?
- Are you somewhat or not at all computer savvy?
- Would you like to be able to use a computer? What is keeping you from beginning the computer adventure?
- Do you send thank-you notes regularly?
- Are you a fair, good, or excellent time-manager?
- Do you plan your day realistically, or do you often have to reschedule or put off appointments?
- Could you make a better living if you were more organized, prompt, efficient, financially stable, or friendly? (Explain.)

- What were your childhood dreams regarding marriage, employment, children, or goals? Have you achieved them? Do you still have those dreams?

The mental area of your life reflects your organizational, financial, and time-management skills. Many of you will find that being meticulous, methodical, neat, and self-controlled are strengths of your personality. Others of you have to work much harder at being disciplined, punctual, or financially prudent. The answers to the above questions allow you to identify the repeated mistakes you make that have become barriers to your success.

Don't be discouraged or disappointed with any of your answers. This is an opportunity to identify certain weaknesses, giving you an awareness of the areas of your life that most need to change.

Listing the Benefits

For every behavior there is a reason. No behavior is purposeless. Before you can change, you must uncover what benefits you are receiving from the negative behavior. For example, if you are overweight, you might be avoiding sex or receiving comfort through food. You may create conflict in your relationships because you're afraid of getting too close to someone and then getting hurt. Your "lack of time" to pursue certain goals guarantees you won't fail because you haven't really tried. Your distance from God might stem from feelings of guilt over something of which you are ashamed.

Identify one habit or behavior in your life that you would like to change.

_____

What are some of the benefits that you have received from holding on to this behavior?

_____

_____

_____

_____

The awareness step in the process of change is a matter of identifying truth, exposing lies, naming barriers, and listing the benefits that you have been receiving from the negative behavior, as well as listing the positive benefits that will be yours if you change!

Listing the positive benefits to changing a specific area of your life can immediately begin to motivate you! Take the same habit that you would like to change and list one or more of the positive benefits that will result from making this change.

_____

_____

If you are still reluctant to give up your negative behaviors, consider the consequences of not changing. Do you really want to live another day of your life with guilt, shame, remorse, anger, resentment, deceit, or fear? What is it that you are holding on to that feels so good but is hurting you and others? Identify the truth about yourself. Expose the lies that you have believed. Name the barriers that have stopped you. And make a list of the benefits.

When you become aware of your need and desire to change,

you are prepared to receive the power to change that comes with admission.

ESSENTIAL STEP #1

Through two very humiliating incidents in the summer of 1976, I became aware that almost every area of my life was out of control. I also learned that when you become aware of something in your life that is hurting you and others, the way out of the lifestyle or deception may not be easy, understood by those closest to you, or as fun as your old life.

The first essential step to overcoming, letting go, healing, or starting over is *becoming aware* of the specific areas in your life that need to change.

TWO

Change Is Empowered by Admission

Simply recognizing your problems does not solve them or make them disappear. If that is all you do, you can remain stuck feeling shameful and hopeless.

That is why, to this day, I am so very grateful that a stranger—a janitor, whose first name is all I can remember—was willing to show me how to take the next step in the process to change my life. He knew that I could not change by my own effort and in secret with only good intentions. I needed outside help. He wisely led me to and through the practical step of admission to myself, to another, and to God so that I would experience the power of forgiveness, as well as be released from guilt and shame that had driven me almost to suicide.

Not only was he the person to whom I confessed every sordid detail of my life, but he connected me with God in a prayer of admission.

First, he told me that God loved me. This overwhelmed me. I didn't think anyone could love me. I didn't even love myself. The concept that I could have a relationship with God became an instant source of power in my courageous fight to become a sober, moral, and fun woman.

Ralph encouraged me to talk out loud to God, to ask Him to forgive me for everything wrong I had ever done. He reassured me that God was forgiving. Ralph's confidence and knowledge of the Bible compelled me to keep listening—despite the little faith I possessed.

With a deep conviction, Ralph told me that God possessed all the power in the world to change me. He said that God—from before all time—had a plan for me. (How did he know that? What kind of purpose could my shattered life ever have?) Ralph urged me to trust God with my life. He told me that God could heal my body and mind and give me a new start—*today*—not *if or when* I was cleaned up and straightened out!

Can you imagine how ready, even desperate, I was to hear such life-changing words? But I wondered how real this "good news" could be. Here was a complete stranger offering me the way to a powerful, immediate, life-changing escape from my shameful addictions.

Interestingly, Ralph didn't ask me to join a religion or a church. He merely suggested that I share my addictions, immorality, and deceitful character in an honest conversation with the living, loving God.

For some reason, I felt comfortable doing this. In fact, I was convinced that talking to God was the best, if not the only thing left that I could do to change the direction of my life.

Even though it was awkward and humiliating in front of Ralph, I lowered my head and vulnerably talked to God about my life. Through streams of tears, I asked Him to forgive me and change me.

The power of God broke through to me. I immediately felt relieved of the shame and guilt I had been carrying. Ralph called this sensation "forgiveness." Immediately, the incessant thoughts of drinking that had been plaguing my mind were gone. They had vanished.

At the end of my prayer, Ralph said, "Becky, your countenance has changed." I didn't even know what he meant until he added, "Your face looks different. The fear and desperation are gone. It has been replaced with peace and love and hope. God lives in you! You have been filled with His Holy Spirit."

In our brief time together, Ralph quoted Bible verses about forgiveness and explained that the supernatural power of God had been released within me. These were all strange and new concepts, but I wasn't afraid or skeptical because of the immediate relief I was beginning to feel.

I no longer craved drugs or alcohol. This was a dramatic change in my mind and body. For weeks and days, even minutes before this encounter with God, I had been anxious, impatient, and fearful about having another drink. Now, I was filled and overflowing with an unexplainable peace. In addition, the erratic emotions that accompanied withdrawal from alcohol were gone.

Ralph simply showed me how to humble myself, to ask God to forgive me. During this prayer, I actually experienced God's forgiveness and unconditional love. It was as if I had taken a very powerful shower that had cleansed my soul and spirit of caked-on mud and dirt. I felt clean. The heaviness in my heart was lifted. My shame was removed.

Before I could change my body and my actions, the overwhelming guilt and shame needed to be released from my mind. That release occurred during the act of admission to another and to God. The power to change followed.

Why Not Change by Yourself?

Is it possible to change without telling anyone you have a problem or need help?

It is possible, but very difficult.

It is possible, but takes longer.

It is possible, but is not as rewarding.

It is possible, but not very probable.

Admission and forgiveness are biblical principles. They are the foundation of a biblical faith, and the essence of the Twelve Steps.

When you "come clean," confess, or publicly acknowledge that you have a problem and need God's help to change, you allow yourself to receive forgiveness in your soul. This is a gift that only God can give to you. No person can offer you *spiritual* healing and cleansing. Admission to God is the step that allows you to receive unconditional love and acceptance.

Although you may have to face those who have not forgiven you or will not accept you, because you have experienced love and forgiveness from God you have courage to no longer hide the truth or lie about your past. You no longer have to pretend to be "okay" when you are not. Transparency and honesty become a positive part of everyday life. So why don't people knock down doors to confess their shortcomings to others, admit their sins to God, and join "honesty" groups for accountability and support?

We have been led to believe that it is better to hide the truth rather than live in the truth. We are convinced that there is too much to lose or too great a price to pay for honesty. We are certain that the truth (or true confession) would damage, rather than restore, our relationships with our spouse, children, employer or ourselves. We consider the consequences of our actions too over-whelming to even think about. We are sure that if we expose our weaknesses, the emotional or financial pain would be too much for those around us to handle.

So we tell no one. We sink deeper. We struggle alone. We grow weary, weak, and more troubled.

Benefits of Admission

I am living proof that holding on to lies, sin, and addiction will steal, kill, and destroy who you are and who you are meant to be! I can offer powerful testimony that on the very day that I "laid it all out" in front of another person to hear and see the ugly truth about me, my life changed for the better. Since that day, I have never turned back to look at my old life with a desire to go back.

Sharing my faults with another person was so humbling that it gave me one more reason to stop the behavior. I *never* again wanted to tell another human being how disgusting I was! It was a positive source of motivation in my recovery.

When I revealed the truth about my addiction, I realized that many of my friends and family members struggled with this same issue. I was just the first to admit it. It didn't make my problems go away, but it gave me the courage to face my addiction. I was a trailblazer for some, a role model for others. In fact, knowing that others were counting on me kept me sober when no one was looking.

However, my confessions did not always receive positive re-sponses or reactions. Nor did being honest about my past make the consequences of my behavior go away. In fact, within a few months, my honesty had cost me my job, social life, and the man I loved.

My coworkers found me less lovable as a sober person. They actually liked me better when I drank, smoked, swore, and had great parties. And they had little interest in my newly professed faith in God.

My party friends no longer found me fun to hang out with, and I found it stressful to hang out with them. When I did go to a party, I carried in—and tightly held onto—a six pack of Dr. Pepper, not giving anyone the opportunity to offer me alcohol, drugs, or cigarettes.

In the beginning stages of sobriety, it was very difficult to have fun and be sober. If I did go to a place full of wildly crazy, loose, and hilariously spontaneous people, I felt left out. It was a constant mental battle to put on a "happy face" around my old friends. It wasn't long before I discovered that I had very little in common with them, especially because I didn't drink. It was very lonely.

The rejection by my boyfriend was an even greater loss. I really loved him and thought that we would get married, but he could not accept that I was an alcoholic. He preferred to think I had a drinking problem, and he counseled me to "just slow down" or to "have only one drink." I knew this advice wouldn't work because from the very first day I drank at age fifteen, I had never had *just one drink!*

Our relationship centered on drinking and dancing together each night after work. He didn't want to lose that part of me. Nor was he willing to quit drinking around me. I seemed to be the only one who could see that drinking was going to destroy me.

Admitting that I was an alcoholic wasn't the only thing that bothered my boyfriend about the "new me." He didn't like the way I talked about God and the Bible all the time. He felt that "religion" was changing me too much, especially our sex life.

In addition to quitting drinking and using drugs, I also moved out of our shared bed and apartment. He was particularly confused about my resolve to no longer have sex with him. He wondered why my new relationship with God had to change this part of our relationship. It became even more frustrating to him when I confidently explained that the Bible said that sex is meant for people who are married. He believed that the Bible was outdated, old-fashioned, not relevant. He felt strongly that people who loved each other should enjoy sex.

I loved him and wanted to be with him. So I asked him, "Why don't we just get married?" Hmm . . . he wanted to have sex with me, live with me, dance with me, but not marry me. It took only a few weeks of sobriety to realize that I had been giving all of my love to someone who was unwilling to—and might never—make a lifetime commitment to me. We had come to an impasse over too many issues. I had changed too much. I was really a different person than the one with whom he had been living before August 26, 1976.

My "true confessions" were more than everyone around me could handle. Those closest to me were unhappy with me.

But I realized that when I publicly confessed my sins, I didn't get rejected from what was good for me. I got pushed away from what was bad for me.

My admission gave me freedom to find emotional healing, physical health, purpose in life, a lifelong soul mate, the courage to be a nurturing mom, and the ability to forgive others.

But the most unexpected and powerful benefit of admission was the love and forgiveness I felt from God. It surrounded me, enveloped me, lifted me, harbored me, carried me, helped me, and changed me for the better. I am convinced that *the turning point* in the process of change is when you admit to yourself, others, *and especially to God* that you desire and need help to change.

Admission to Self

When you admit to yourself that you need to change, you accept responsibility for your behavior.

Take the time, before reading on, to answer the following list of questions that are designed to help you admit the truth to yourself in all four areas of your life: physical, emotional, spiritual, and mental.

PHYSICAL

- Do you agree that regular weekly exercise is essential for a healthy body?
- Could you find thirty to sixty minutes a day, three or four days of the week, to exercise? If you can't find a block of thirty minutes, can you find three ten-minute or two fifteen-minute blocks?
- What foods do you love but know are not healthy for you? Could you accept having them as occasional treats only?
- Do you have any physical or medical conditions that restrict you from any or all forms of exercise? Will you accept those restrictions and at the same time find alternate exercises?
- Can you accept that there is an area of your body, such as big or small bones, height, or inherited traits such as thick ankles, small bust size, large foot or hand size, etc., that will not change through eating right and exercising regularly?

(If you will accept that you are uniquely made, it will relieve undue anxiety over trying to change areas of your life that cannot change naturally.)

EMOTIONAL

- Are you in an unhealthy relationship in which you are lowering your standards, being abused, having to lie, etc.?
- Are you willing to take responsibility for a problem, rather than shift blame to another?
- Are you willing to accept that a relationship may never change, but you will be much healthier if you can forgive the person and move on?
- Are you willing to see giving as a positive human characteristic that must be developed in your life in order to become a more complete and fulfilled person?
- Are you unforgiving? (Can you name anyone that you don't want to talk to? If so, there is your answer.)

SPIRITUAL

- Do you accept that there is a God who loves you?
- Do you accept that He desires to be in a relationship with you?
- Do you accept that there is immense and intense fullness of life available when you pursue spiritual growth?
- Are you willing to accept the responsibility and challenge to know God better?
- Are you willing to make time for God in your life every day? If not, why not? If so, how?

MENTAL

- Do you procrastinate, or are you regularly late? Ask those around you if they have ever waited for you more than five minutes. Ask your coworkers if they can depend on you to keep a deadline.
- Would you agree that a daily appointment with yourself (with journal, Bible, and calendar) will improve your ability to accomplish the things you have said that you will do?
- Do you accept that your current problems with time management are partially based on your past experiences and background? Are you willing to name any bad habits (such as procrastination, tardiness, avoidance, laziness, etc.) and begin to move away from them so that you will be a more productive and happy, healthy person?
- What are your greatest emotional weaknesses that could hinder you from completing a project? (Examples: impatience, laziness, fear of failure, pride, ego, selfishness, or jealousy)
- Can you identify the most obvious distractions that keep you from completing tasks and focusing on a project? (Examples: TV, telephone, social engagements)

Until you become honest with yourself, you will resist being honest with others.

Admitting to Others

Let me be the first to assure you that it is a most humbling experience to reveal the truth about yourself to others. It is equally humbling to admit that you have fallen short of someone's expectations of you. And sometimes other's reactions to your admission are hurtful and disappointing. But admission is the nonnegotiable step that allows you to experience complete wholeness and healing. It takes you from the darkness of secrets and shame and opens the door to true emotional and spiritual freedom that is found in honesty and transparency.

In the New Testament, James 5:16 says, "Confess your sins to one another . . . *so that you may be healed*" (NLT). The Bible promises that when you admit to others that you have been wrong, acknowledge how you have hurt them, and ask them to forgive you—in addition to all that it does for others—*you* begin to heal. This has certainly been true in my life.

Each time I have come to a place where my life is out of control, or I have accumulated too much emotional baggage to go on, the turning point has been an admission of my wrong. In each case, I can point to my "confession" experience—as in 1976 with Ralph the janitor—as the last time I repeated a certain behavior, held tightly to something that was self-destructive, or continued undesirable habits. The acts of admission to myself, to another, and to God were the moments when healing was released in my life.

That is why I am not embarrassed or ashamed to tell my story in public. In front of as few as one and as many as forty thousand people, I have told the details of my embarrassing and painful past. I willingly expose the ugly truth about who I was and what I did, and I boldly tell the story of my confession to the janitor and to God *because* it is through this step that I received positive help and powerful emotional healing to change. Through my transparency, people have become aware of and are more willing to admit that they need to make certain changes in their lives. And when they hear my entire story they can see that there is new life after admitting the truth about oneself! (In fact, the potential for a wonderful life is unlimited!)

How does admission to another person lift you out of your pain and problems and empower you to change? By telling another person (or a group) that you are struggling with something or someone, you no longer pretend that the situation is harmless or nonexistent. By admission, you open yourself up to another's response, insight, advice, or rebuke. You can't be sure what their reaction to your confession might be, but if you have a safe place, a trusted friend, or a small group of fellow sojourners to be honest with, you have the opportunity to share your problems with objective, friendly supporters. (In Chapter Eight, accountability to a group is explained in detail.)

It is equally important to be patient and understand that only time will heal certain wounds and relationships. In fact, it is not mandatory that you openly confess your weaknesses to those whom you have hurt. They may not be alive, or perhaps they are remarried, or there are other circumstances that would make open confession inappropriate.

Often, just knowing that you have told one or many others that you are going to make certain amends or changes will motivate, prompt, encourage, and inspire you to follow through when nothing else has worked!

Admitting to God

I am convinced that if people would have an *encounter* with the living, loving God, they would be compelled to know Him better, receive His love, and tell others about His healing power. That is why I strongly believe that everyone needs someone who will listen to their confession, not be their judge, and show them how to humbly talk to (and "get right with") God.

Ralph the janitor had nothing to gain and everything to lose by offering me the power to change. When he suggested that I admit any sins to God (in front of him), I could have rejected the idea as too embarrassing or rationalized that my behavior was common to my generation and times. But Ralph pressed me to talk to God, to be honest, and to ask God to forgive me. He knew that a cleansing of the shame and guilt that had been saturating and darkening my heart and my mind was on the other side of the humbling prayer.

Ralph was the person who introduced me to the living, loving God. He was brave! He knew his message wasn't the popular, feel good, "you can do it" approach to life. He knew that I could have shut him out because of "God" talk.

But Ralph looked past all of those obstacles because *he* had been met and changed by God. And he wanted *me* to have a life-changing encounter with God.

Up until August 26, 1976, I equated God with religion. As a child, I went to church every single Sunday with my family. When I left home at seventeen, I quit attending church. I thought I knew a lot about God. What I realized that day with Ralph is that although I understood certain things about religion, I did not understand that I could be in a relationship with God.

My years of childhood Bible training put me in touch with my most vivid pictures of a loving God. I had been taught, and history validates, that there was a person whose name is Jesus of Nazareth who came to earth, lived a perfect life, died by crucifixion, and rose from the dead. He was the perfect sacrifice who "washed away the sins of the world."

On that day with Ralph I understood that I was an imperfect

human being, a sinner, who was separated from a holy and perfect God and needed a Savior. I realized that God loved me. God showed His love to me through the sacrifice of His one and only Son. And Jesus showed His love for me by dying for my sins, when I didn't even know or love Him.

I understood that admitting every shameful thing to God was an agreement with Him that I was indeed a sinner. It was my acknowledgment that I was ready to turn from those destructive, though previously satisfying, habits to follow Him.

I surely didn't anticipate the incredible wave of relief from guilt and shame that flooded my heart and mind immediately following my honest and sincere confession to God. At the time, I didn't realize fully that humbling myself before God was the pathway to experiencing forgiveness and healing, and to complete wholeness and happiness. But I immediately sensed that the admission of my sin had ushered me into a new and personal relationship with the living, loving God.

I will be forever grateful that there was someone on this earth who could see the potential for change within me without judging me by who I was up to that point. More than likely, anyone who knew me would have been understandably reluctant to suggest that God could forgive and love me. Yet this stranger embodied the compassion that Søren Kierkegaard spoke of: "Never cease loving a person, and never give up hope for him, for even the prodigal son who had fallen most low, could still be saved."

Because I was so dramatically and profoundly changed by the willingness of a janitor to show me the way to God, from that day forward I have had an endless, enthusiastic passion to be the "janitor" in someone else's life!

In fact, just last night, a woman whom I have known for many years called me. She had been through a period of running from

God that resulted in much personal embarrassment, physical infirmity, and emotional pain. Although many she knew could have rightly expressed disappointment in her, I knew why she chose to call me. She knew my story. I, too, had been almost hopelessly lost at one time. She was hoping to find someone to pray with her, alleviate her pain, and ultimately lead her back to God.

I had to speak the truth in love. I said, "If you want God to heal you and change you, you must first be willing to admit to Him where you have been wrong. Would you be willing to do that?" She was extremely willing, not one bit reluctant.

I empathized with her level of despair. I had been there. I marveled at her transparency. And I understood the freedom that she was longing to experience—the spiritual cleansing that only God could give her. With each prayer of admission and confession, she hurriedly offered up another, saying, "I want to get all of this out of me. I don't want to live like this anymore."

I love being the messenger who says, "God loves you just the way you are." I feel privileged to lead people in a prayer where they can honestly admit their shortcomings, struggles, failings, bad habits, and, yes, sins, to God. I love to tell others of the truth found in the Bible: if they confess their sins, they will receive healing in their relationships, relief from their shame and guilt, forgiveness of sin, and find a loving Savior waiting to change their lives—now, and for eternity.

After twenty-two years of sobriety, fidelity within my marriage, successful motherhood, and a career of helping others, I am living proof that this step of admission will absolutely change your life *for the better.*

ESSENTIAL STEP #2
When you admit to yourself and others that you have a problem, you expose the truth about yourself and signal to those around

you that you are serious about your desire to change. This begins to heal you.

When you admit to God that you need and want to change, you are cleansed and forgiven. What He releases within you, although invisible, empowers you to do what you cannot do without His help!

Admission is the verbal, outward sign of an inward decision to turn from a bad habit, destructive pattern, or unhealthy relationship.

Awareness and admission begin the process and release the power to change. But to achieve long-lasting change, it is imperative to follow a written, daily action plan.

THREE

Change Is Achieved Through a Daily Action Plan

By the time I was twenty-nine years old, I was known in my community as an adult who cared a lot about teenagers. I volunteered many hours in the public high school as a coach, mentor, and youth worker. Each year, for over five years, I coached fifty cheerleaders. I was responsible for running daily practices, attending games twice each weekend, and coordinating pep rallies, summer camps, and fundraisers, not to mention the hours it took to manage fifty high-school girls.

In addition, I was the club director for the local high school Campus Life club, which averaged seventy-five students in weekly attendance. As the club director I was also a spiritual mentor and trainer to at least ten college-aged students who volunteered to help me run the citywide club meetings. I was married to the executive director of the Campus Life program in Cleveland, which required me to attend many board meetings and staff functions.

I was also the mother of a toddler. At that time, day care

wasn't affordable or preferable, so I worked out of my home, arranging my schedule and commitments around my son. He went with me to the after-school games and practices, and my parents lived close enough to watch him during most of my evening meetings and games.

On the outside, I seemed to be a very productive woman who had it all together, but I was a completely disorganized, selfish wife and a screaming, impatient mother. I harbored a number of resentments and quickly lashed out in anger at anyone who hurt or offended me. I was stubborn and selfish in my closest relationships. I seemed unable to manage money, and I allowed jealousy and unforgiveness to undermine many of my relationships. I would overeat, or never eat, and could not find time to exercise, even though I was very athletic. I am embarrassed to add that I was an overweight workaholic who was envious of her size-five cheerleaders.

A closer look would have revealed that my life was out of control—and in the very same ways it had been out of control when I was an addict! The tell-tale sign was that I was not the same person in private that I was in public. In front of my cheerleaders, I appeared to be kind and personable, but I struggled not to use a mean word toward or about another. In the privacy of my home, I could easily erupt with anger, especially at my child. In my mind, I daily compared myself to those who were thinner and richer than me. Though I acted as if I was happy with my weight, I began to eat less and less. And though parents spoke admirably of my dedication to the hundreds of teens I coached and mentored, I resented having no free time for myself.

By February of 1984, it was not *one* area in my life or a glaring, obvious weakness that made me aware that I needed to change, but rather the growing awareness that *every* area of my life was spinning out of control. I could no longer act as if I led a wonderful life of fulfillment in service to others. There were just too many days that I just wasn't at peace with the woman I was, the mom or wife I was, or with the workaholic way I was living and working. I was sick of the emotional drain that it took to pretend. I was discouraged and disappointed in myself.

Even though I appeared on the outside to have it together (a common trait of compulsive, addictive people), I was unraveling on the inside. My life was unmanageable and out of balance in every area: weight, finances, spirituality, relationships, and emotions.

At that juncture, I was scheduled to attend an annual youth worker's conference in Chicago. The timing for a getaway was perfect. I decided that this would be an event where I would reflect, re-evaluate, and refocus—and come home a new woman!

Reflection, Reevaluation, Refocus

While on the drive to Chicago, I pondered my past experiences, searching for some explanation for my present state of disarray. I wondered where my previous strength, bubbly joy, and love for students—and God—had gone. I recalled the passion that had erupted within me when I first began my personal relationship with God. It had been revolutionary. It had changed my entire life.

Further reflection showed me that each year I had added more responsibilities and relationships to my life. In the process of *doing* and *planning* and *leading*, I had lost my focus and purpose. I had become so busy *doing* good things, I didn't notice that my life had slipped out of control physically, emotionally, spiritually, and mentally.

Just as it had happened eight years earlier, I had an over-whelming sense that my life was out of control. Only this time, I was even more disappointed in myself because I was a leader who did not live by the principles I taught others!

As the hours passed in the van, I began to chat with a new friend whose husband was a board member of Cleveland Campus Life. I shared with Kinney my expectation that something posi-tive might come out of this week away from home. In fact, we discussed what life "after youth work" might look like. I secretly wanted to build a consensus that this out-of-control life was a result of overworking, not inner weakness. I wanted to get off the merry-go-round of workaholism and retire.

Once we arrived at the convention, we were all excited to hear the wonderful lineup of speakers, all former presidents of the organization. I couldn't help but think that one of their speeches would give me a quick solution or the "easy out" for which I was searching.

I was completely overwhelmed by the content of the powerful keynote messages. Instead of a variety of inspirational talks, there was a theme that threaded through the event. It was this: the sign of a relevant faith is that—over time—it will continue to change your life *for the better.*

Through each message, I began to see myself as one who had *once* experienced a dramatic change, and then somewhere along the way, I quietly proceeded to stop changing. The evidence for this was not only seen in my outward appearance and actions but also found in my internal discontent.

Instead of being motivated by an inner call to work with stu-dents, I was feeling trapped, burned out, and overcommitted. Rather than reacting with patience or kindness, I was continually struggling simply to be nice! It was easier for me to lose control of my temper than to remain in control of my emotions. And it was probably no secret that I was envious of others' successes by my unwillingness to delegate.

I was desperate for change, but because so many aspects of my life needed revision, I had no idea where to begin. One thing was certain: I was ready and willing to take *any* step and make *any* change that would bring relief to my discouragement and significant improvement to my life.

I simply did not want to go home to my son, husband, cheerleaders, volunteers, and parents as the irritable, angry, overweight, disorganized person who had left them.

By the end of the first day, I realized that I needed more than a convention high to get back on track. I was going to have to accept where I was, take a serious look at which areas of my life needed to change, and develop and follow a long-term plan for making those changes.

At first I was discouraged because I knew firsthand how difficult it was to make a complete life change because of my own previous battle with alcoholism. In addition, I was daily involved with students who were finding it very hard to change or improve one or more areas of their lives. Attempting to change was the primary pursuit of everyone I knew. I personally experienced and daily observed people who fought hard, often, and long to change. But I was fully aware that my repeated excuses and undisciplined efforts had caused me to waste my God-given talents and squander my potential for success. I was finally ready to do whatever it took to stop the unraveling and start turning into a physically, emotionally, mentally, and spiritually whole and healthy woman.

But the question of how to change so many aspects of my life lingered. What could I do right now? What was missing in my life?

I was certainly making a difference in other's lives. My days were filled full, if not overly full, of doing good things. I was a visible community leader; a spiritual mentor who gave advice, counsel, and speeches on spiritual growth and balanced living.

That night, I reflected on what had changed my life so dramatically in 1976. How had I made huge strides away from a lifestyle of addiction? I realized that not only had I surrounded myself with new friends and avoided certain places, but there had been one specific activity that had given me an incredible amount of courage and confidence to change.

In those beginning days of struggling to achieve sobriety and morality, my problems seemed so obvious. I was in so much need of a supernatural power to help me to get through each day that I had been very diligent about spending time daily alone with God. I would regularly read the Bible, searching for practical wisdom on how to make right decisions. I would talk to Him about my anxieties, obstacles, fears, emotions, physical addictions, and jealousies, *no matter where I was or what I was doing.* In 1976, I was convinced that I could not manage my daily life without God's help.

Now, in 1984, as a leader and mentor to others, I was proud that I no longer struggled with the "sins" of drugs or alcohol or immorality. But in the process of achieving sobriety, I neglected to see emotional weaknesses, such as jealousy, anger, and unforgiveness, as sins in my life. I considered these characteristics to be bad habits, rather than self-destructive patterns that had the power to take over my emotional life and undermine most of my relationships.

A more careful and honest examination of my life would have revealed that my life was out of balance physically because of many unresolved issues. The emotionally unhealthy way that I dealt with anger undermined any attempt I made to develop healthy exercise and eating habits. My tendency to overcommit and to schedule appointments and meetings too tightly promoted more disorganization in my day-to-day life, resulting in poor time and financial management. All of this affected my relationships with God and others.

Unlike in 1976, I could not blame a specific action or addiction for my present out-of-control life. But I was every bit as desperate to find some positive step that I could take to radically change my life—*before* I left the convention.

I decided to attend a Saturday optional workshop on prayer. If you knew me then, you would have been as surprised as my friend Kinney was at this decision. I am not a serious person. I love to laugh, have fun, and be entertained. So how exciting was a two-hour prayer workshop going to be? It was a tough decision to attend a meeting that might be boring, but I told her that I thought *God* wanted me to go to the workshop. I felt pulled into that room.

During the workshop, I listened to the presenter talk about prayer as a two-way conversation with God. This concept chipped away at my current attitude about prayer. I considered prayer to be a very boring, quiet discipline for elderly people and clergy. This speaker made "time with God" sound exciting, an inviting, powerful experience that was an adventure waiting to happen. I wanted that kind of daily spiritual experience in my life. I wanted to have an exciting, expectant faith, as when I first encountered God.

So I decided to do something that would catapult me from a "do-gooder's" life to living life in an adventure with the living, loving God.

I wanted to be sure that someone would later remind me that this moment of decision was not simply a figment of my imagination, so I asked a woman I hardly knew to pray with me. In a short prayer, I made a non-negotiable decision to spend one hour *every day for the rest of my life talking to God and listening to Him.* I actually had no idea *how* I was going to do this, but I was determined to follow through.

Upon returning home from the convention, I set the alarm clock to wake me the next morning at 6:00 A.M. in order to have my first "one-hour appointment" with God. (I led such a full and busy life that there was no other uninterrupted hour in my day.)

I had often seen my husband journal, so upon waking up, I got out an old three-ringed notebook with plenty of ruled paper. For one hour that morning—with notebook, Bible, and a pot of coffee—I proceeded to write out my prayers, dreams, hopes, struggles, and anxieties to God. It was a refreshing feeling to entrust my thoughts to God so freely. I hadn't been so transparent with Him for a very long time. When I was done writing, I read familiar verses in the Bible and wrote down the verses that were particularly meaningful to me. These written conversations became the record of my conversations with God and His responses to me.

I immediately sensed that God was meeting with me, that He had things He wanted to tell me. In fact, I got the impression that He had been waiting a long time to get my undivided attention. I would jealously guard my daily appointments with God, seeing them as the time and place where He would advise, correct, direct, answer, and give me hope. My relationship with God found a new depth through the journal experience. Just as the workshop speaker had promised, prayer became my two-way conversation with Someone who loved me.

I Discovered Prayer, Decided to Pray, and Designed a Prayer Journal . . .

I quickly discovered that prayer was not a spiritual discipline intended only for serious, theological people. I saw prayer as the method that human beings were given not only to communicate with the unseen, and very real, living, loving God but also to find their purpose in life. And the longer I maintained the discipline of writing my prayers, the clearer and stronger my purpose in life grew. In addition, as I read through the Bible each day, I saw how God—in a variety of ways—gave instructions to people. His will and plan for each of us were not meant to be elusive or unattainable but found through daily communication with Him!

I had stumbled onto a practical method for talking to God and listening to Him. Journaling my two-way conversations with God took the mystery out of the concept of prayer and meditation and made it real. As I began to write my specific needs and requests to God, I received answers!

Within three months of making the decision to spend one hour a day with God for the rest of my life, I designed a journaling tool and began to enthusiastically share it with my friends, cheerleaders, Campus Life kids, and volunteers.

The prayer journal, called *My Partner Prayer Notebook,* has ten sections for talking to God and listening to God.

In the Praise section, I used the Psalms as my patterns for prayer. I discovered that the Psalms have been the place where, for centuries, people have learned to pray. And although they were once unfamiliar to me, for the past fifteen years I have read through the Book of Psalms each month. They remind me that written prayer is not a new idea!

I also have an Admit section in my journal where I *daily* discuss why I am not at peace with myself, others, or God. My commitment is to ask God—every twenty-four hours—to reveal to me the areas of my life that are "out of control." This is the simple method I use to become *aware* of the areas in my life that are susceptible to temptation, denial, or selfishness. In my journal, I talk to God about where I am at with certain issues, who or what I am struggling with, and what doesn't feel right. I admit where I am wrong, and I ask God to forgive me and help me to change.

In the Request section, I keep a list of names and specific issues or events where I am asking God to help, intervene, or heal. For fifteen years, I have prayed through the many pages in this section, recording how and when God answers.

The last section where I talk to God is called Thanks. Every day, I thank God for the small and big ways in which I can see that He is touching my life.

In the next five sections of my prayer notebook, I become a listener, rather than a talker. In the Listening section, I write down thoughts that come to my mind and heart during meditative moments. I usually write down a verse from the Bible that I have memorized. The Message section is the place where I take notes of talks, lessons, and sermons that inspire, encourage, and teach me more about God. In the sections called New Testament, Old Testament, and Proverbs, I record meaningful verses that I read out of the version of the Bible that I use, which is called **The change your life Daily Bible.** It is the entire Bible divided into 365 daily readings of a few New and Old Testament chapters, a Psalm, and one or two verses from the Book of Proverbs.

A To Do section is the final section in *My Partner Prayer Notebook* where I make a list of anything that I should do later but that has come to mind during the hour when I am praying and reading my Bible.

This journal experience made the concept of prayer a tangible activity for me and for others. As my enthusiasm for this new habit grew, I began to teach others, young and old, how to talk to God and listen to God using this method. This simple style of communicating with God caught on so rapidly that it wasn't long before I was invited to travel all over the United States to teach people how to connect daily with God through journaling!

> *We make decisions, and then turn around
> and the decisions make us.*
> F. W. BORCHAM

By 1995, I had lectured in almost every state in America to hundreds of thousands of people of all ages, races, and denominations on how to "let prayer change your life."

About that time, I began to see a trend. People wanted to learn more about prayer. They did not simply want to find spiritual balance but were looking for healing and harmony in *every* aspect of their lives and relationships.

Married couples, students, and singles were becoming aware that their lives were spinning out of control. Marriages were falling apart at an alarming rate. Students were drifting away from wholesome desires and falling deeper into violence, sexual experimentation, and substance abuse. And singles of all ages were finding it harder to find people of like values, morals, and spiritual convictions to love and marry.

Everywhere I spoke, people would come up to me during the breaks and tearfully confess their deepest sins, and admit that they needed and wanted God's help to change. Although they embraced a faith in the living, loving God, they were completely frustrated with their inability to achieve long-lasting change with their eating and exercise goals, family priorities, or in overcoming their emotional weaknesses. Most significantly, they simply could not seem to integrate their spirituality into every area of their lives.

And although they expressed the need and desire for a daily action plan, they confessed that they didn't have a lot of time in their busy, overwhelmed lives.

Journaling—A Written Daily Action Plan

I knew that journaling could change people's lives, and I was determined to design a journaling tool that would truly help people achieve a healthy body, heal their relationships, connect with God, and make it all happen—one day at a time.

By this time, I had spent over four thousand one-hour daily encounters with God. When I reflected back on my written conversations, I discovered that praying for one hour every day had not *just* changed me spiritually. My daily appointment with God was the place where I received the daily action plan for changing *every* area of my life.

PHYSICALLY

Before I had hourly, daily appointments with God, I was haphazard in my workout attempts, a yo-yo dieter, inconsistent, and obsessive. When I began to journal, I talked to God about my appetite, laziness, and what changes I desired, and I asked Him to help me.

During the first year that I journaled every day, I dropped a few dress sizes, found a comfortable weight, and maintained it for the next few years. By the fifth year until the present, I have maintained my ideal weight of 125 pounds. In addition, for every year that I have prayed for one hour a day, I have exercised an average of three times a week, a minimum requirement for reducing weight or maintaining a desired weight.

Now, each year, my husband says I look younger and more fit than the year before. I honestly attribute my consistent discipline to eat right and exercise regularly to my daily conversations with God!

EMOTIONALLY

As a result of my hourly appointments with God, I began to experience incredible emotional healing in many of my relationships. One noticeable change was found on page after page of my journal where I began to ask God to change *me,* rather than the other person. This was certainly an "about-face" in my attitude. I also asked Him to help me forgive people whom I had been too stubborn to forgive. And not a day went by when I didn't have to ask Him to give me strength not to shout, courage not to resent, and a transparent honesty in my relationship with Him and others. I've come a long way, and I still desire to change and grow.

SPIRITUALLY

At one time, I would have considered spiritual disciplines such as fasting and extended times of prayer and meditation too difficult for me to master. But over time and after many conversations with God, my concept of my "spiritual" self has changed.

Because of the practical methods I have used to improve my

spiritual growth, I have systematically read through the Bible each year for over ten years. To read any book every day for ten years takes a considerable amount of consistency and discipline. Words such as those certainly did not describe me before I began to pray for an hour a day, but they have become a part of who I am with each passing year.

In addition, what I daily read in the Bible causes me to *want to* know God better, love Him more, and to make Him known. In fact, I have impacted hundreds of thousands of people since I began to journal my prayers, encouraging them to have a daily encounter with God!

MENTALLY

Mentally, many of the goals and plans that were once only dreams in my heart became reality after daily discussions with God. I still lose my keys, but I am no longer disorganized, tardy, or a woman in debt. I've successfully pursued professional aspirations such as owning my own company, producing fitness videos, registering a trademark and service mark, self-publishing, incorporating, designing a Web site, employing a staff, and acquiring aerobic certification. All of these projects took time, energy, organization, and focus. Anyone who knew me fifteen years ago would agree that I did not possess the ability to follow through and achieve such goals on my own.

Through daily encounters with God, I received a daily, step-by-step "blueprint" for each project, a "to do" list for the day, and confidence to move forward when no one else encouraged me or believed in my dream.

Journaling my thoughts, hopes, confessions, dreams, and requests to God changed me physically, emotionally, spiritually, and mentally. Because all four areas of my life had changed, improved, and balanced because of the journaling, I knew that if I could make journaling a practical and simple activity, more people would be inclined to give it a try.

During a summer-long effort of prayer, fasting, and brainstorming, I contemplated a "change your life" daily action plan. I asked myself one specific question: "What are the practical things that I do every day that are a result of my journal time?" I discovered that life-long change is not achieved by focusing solely on one area of life, but by caring about, working on, and balancing all four areas of one's life. Incredibly, I found that by just focusing *daily* on two simple concepts in each life area— physical, emotional, spiritual, and mental—I could radically improve my relationships, find and fulfill my life purpose, see positive physical changes, restore my emotional health, and increase my spirituality.

Determined to come up with a daily journal system that was simple enough for anyone to do yet powerful enough to bring change into anyone's life, I developed a daily, written action plan that includes 8 Daily To Do's: **Eating Right** and **Exercising Regularly** (physical); **Forgiving** and **Giving** (emotional); **Talking to God** and **Listening to God** (spiritual); and **Detailing Your Day** and **Defining Your Dreams** (mental).

The change your life Daily Journal is a twenty- to thirty-minute journal experience during which you daily record your 8 Daily To Do's on four balanced life journal pages. Each page has two Daily To Do's that bring accountability, organization, and balance into the physical, emotional, spiritual, and mental areas of your life.

How It Works . . .

At almost every event, I quote John L. Beckley, who said, "Most people don't plan to fail; they fail to plan." In order to change your life, I am going to ask you to make a daily appointment with *yourself* in your own journal or in **The change your life Daily Journal.**

On each journal page, you will be required to record your plans, intentions, hopes, deepest desires, thoughts, goals, and dreams. My only request is that you make a *daily* entry on each of the four balanced life pages and transfer any appointments or to do's to the Calendar page of **The change your life Daily Journal** or the calendar section of your daily organizer.

I believe that your ability to see your life change is dependent upon your daily commitment to journal in each of the four balanced life pages—no matter how comfortable or uncomfortable this may be to you. Like the successful basketball coach Rick Pitino, I have found that to achieve your goals "you have to make your New Year's Resolutions 365 days a year. The same resolve. The same determination. The same commitment. And do it on a daily basis."

Each balanced life page is divided into two daily to do's that will give you two practical ways to record how you will change your life today. On the **Physical** journal page, you will record how you daily intend to **Eat Right** and **Exercise Regularly**. You will also be asked to think about any obstacles that you may face each day and develop ways to overcome them. On the **Emotional** journal page, you have an opportunity to daily **Forgive** and **Give**. These are two actions that will bring healing to your emotions and relationships. I like to call the **Emotional** page "the Twelve Steps in two steps." On the **Spiritual** journal page, you are given journal space to **Talk to God** and **Listen to God.** By using a Bible that is divided into 365 days, such as **The change your life Daily Bible**, you have the ability to daily read and hear God's voice through His written word. This will take away a magical approach to listening to God and provide you with a practical method for having a daily encounter with God. And on the **Mental** journal page, you are encouraged to **Detail Your Day** on a simple, practical "to do" list. There is also space on this page to **Define Your Dream** in daily steps.

In the next four chapters, I will show you how a daily action plan—that is based on journaling—will bring balance and change into all four areas of your life. You can experience how to *tend to body basics* by eating right and exercising regularly; *heal and be healed* by forgiving and giving; *connect with God,* by talking and listening to Him; and *make it happen* by detailing your day and defining your dreams—in writing!

ESSENTIAL STEP #3

The third essential step that I took to achieve change in every area of my life was to follow a daily action plan where I had an appointment with God and myself—in writing—for a non-negotiable amount of time every day.

My decision to . . .
journal my conversations with God,
confess my shortcomings to Him and others,
discuss my ideas and dreams and goals with God,
work through my daily schedule,
ask God to specifically help me and others,
listen for His voice to speak back to me through the Bible, and
quiet myself for one hour a day for the past fifteen years of my
life has changed every area of my life—one day at a time.

date _____

eat right

- · understand your own body type, genetics, metabolism, etc.
- · design a healthy, "plan ahead" eating plan that includes a balance
  of all the food groups in moderate portions
- · **record your daily intentions for meals and snacks below**
- · **review your progress and make daily adjustments**

breakfast _____

_____

lunch _____

_____

dinner _____

_____

snacks _____

_____

exercise regularly

- · determine what type of activity, where, when, how often and with whom you
  most like to exercise
- · develop a "week at a glance" exercise plan that includes a variety of 3 to 4 activities
  and has provision for alternate dates and times.

Detail your week plan; highlight today's plan.... what? when? where? with whom?

sun	mon	tue	wed	thur	fri	sat

journal

**Journal below about any temptations, circumstances or emotions—today—
that might keep you from reaching your goals?** (ex: vacation, celebrations, etc.)

_____

_____

_____

_____

_____

_____

p
h
y
s
i
c
a
l

change
your
life
daily

date _____

e

m

o

t

i

o

n

a

l

forgive

To experience emotional balance on a daily basis, allow one or more of the below questions to prompt you to journal about the relationships in your life that need to heal and be healed.

Today, I know I need to ask _____ **to forgive me.**

I need to forgive myself for _____

I need to forgive _____ **for** _____

And I ask God to forgive me for _____

_____

_____

_____

_____

_____

_____

_____

What additional step(s) can I take to complete the healing that I have just journaled about in the above space? (ex: a phone call, letter, apology, etc.)

_____

_____

_____

_____

give

The gift of time, money, resources, or talent to an organization or person is both a powerful and practical way to help others.
What need comes to my mind—today—that I can find and fill and/or what person or organization needs a specific source of comfort or encouragement that I can give?

_____

_____

_____

_____

_____

_____

change
your
life
daily

date _____

talk to God

Today, in honest transparency, share—in writing—your thoughts, gratitude, regrets, fears, plans, hopes, dreams and requests for yourself and others with the living, loving God.

_____
_____
_____
_____
_____
_____
_____
_____
_____
_____
_____
_____
_____
_____
_____
_____
_____
_____
_____

s
p
i
r
i
t
u
a
l

listen to God

God's voice is found in His word, the Bible.
Unless you have another system, read today's **change your life** Daily Bible using Today's Date. Write in this area, any verse or verses that stand out, touch your heart, encourage or correct you. **What is God saying to you today?**

_____
_____
_____
_____
_____
_____
_____

change
your
life
daily

date _____

m
e
n
t
a
l

detail your day

appointments

quiet time	☐
work out	☐
	☐
	☐
	☐
	☐
	☐
	☐
	☐
	☐
	☐
	☐
	☐
	☐
	☐
	☐
	☐

calls to make   *phone #*

letters to write/fax/email
w f e
☐ ☐ ☐
☐ ☐ ☐
☐ ☐ ☐
☐ ☐ ☐

things to do

☐
☐
☐
☐
☐

define your dream

What is one practical step you can take toward reaching a goal—
and fulfilling a dream—in one or more areas of your life?
Use this space to brainstorm or to develop a dream that won't go away!

physical | emotional
mental | spiritual

change
your
life
daily

I believe that no matter how broken your life or how large or small your secret and shameful habits, you can *change your destructive patterns and sinful traits. By having a daily action plan that encourages journaling and records your progress, you can achieve a healthy body, improve your relationships, and connect with God.*

FOUR

Tend to Body Basics (Physical)

Eat Right
Exercise Regularly

BENEFIT: *Eating Right and Exercising Regularly affects appearance, attitudes, & activity/energy level.*

TRUTH: *Every person is different; one program does not work for everyone. Understanding your body type, metabolism, and genetics allows you to design a successful and personalized fitness strategy that can be achieved through a daily, written action plan.*

If you have struggled to maintain a certain weight and eat healthy every day, or been haphazard in your attempt to exercise regularly, you are not alone in the battle to change, improve, or balance the physical area of your life. Striving to be physically fit may very well be the most common, shared struggle of American men and women today.

I know very few people who do not desire to exercise more consistently or improve their eating habits. If there are a fortunate few who have *never* had to work out or watch what they eat, I haven't met one of them yet, and I am certainly not one of them! Throughout my teens and twenties, I struggled with inconsistent exercise patterns and was always tempted to try the newest fad diet.

It took me quite a few years, but by the time I was thirty, I finally discovered how to maintain a physically fit body. It was not found in a secret solution, pill, through starvation methods, or extreme exercise, although I had tried all of those. I was able to find balance and improve my fitness level by both accepting what I could not change about my body (my unique genetic and inherited traits) and making it a priority to tend to body basics *every* day of my life.

I believe that this change in attitude and action occurred because of my daily journal appointments. Each day I would journal about the most pressing concerns of my heart and mind. Hardly a day went by when I did not journal about my struggle to get the physical area of my life in balance. It was through my journal pages that I began to identify my inconsistent eating and exercise patterns and became honest about my lazy excuses. Most significant, I articulated—over and over—that I desired to become healthy, athletic, and fit, rather than an overweight, non-active human.

I determined to find a way to bring my heart's desires to a point of agreement with my body. The spiritual strength that I had developed through journaling and praying gave me the necessary courage and discipline to believe that, with God's help, I could make my body do what my heart and mind wanted it to do. Because I had seen many bad habits in my life reversed or changed because of journaling, I considered this activity to be my most important step in developing an overall plan to balance the physical area of my life. In addition, I began to read books and articles based on medical studies, which gave practical advice for achieving and maintaining a healthy body.

The most general of research showed that eating right and exercising regularly are the two basic activities that we must incorporate into our daily lives in order to achieve a healthy body. Physicians, nutritionists, and fitness professionals recommended a *daily* plan that included both of these components as the most practical way to increase one's overall health and fitness. They also warned that neglect of one's physical health could result in health problems that ranged from improper nutrition to obesity, heart problems, or even severe eating disorders.

Although most people would agree that eating right and exercising regularly are the ideal ways to achieve a healthy body, these two components appear to be the very stumbling blocks to our success. Almost every man or woman who wants to reduce two or more inches off of his/her waistline or lose five, ten, or more pounds will admit that they would much rather do it without much sacrifice, sweat, or hard work—and in the minimum amount of time. More of us have done the work that it takes to lose weight or inches, only to turn around and regain what was lost. And how many of us have *never* been able to follow an eating or exercise plan for more than a few days or at best a week? But even those who are convinced that the best formula for reducing weight or inches is to follow a disciplined plan of eating less, cutting back on fat and excess sugar, and increasing activity levels, have found that this elementary plan is nearly impossible to follow. Millions of people in the pursuit of a healthy body fail miserably.

Why do we consistently fail to achieve change and balance in the physical area of our lives? It is certainly not for lack of money or ideas. I contend that it is because we have not accepted that a healthy body is the result of a lifelong process of eating right and exercising regularly. We are simply unrealistic—or perhaps in denial—about the amount of time and consistent attention that it takes to achieve a noticeable change in our body shape and size.

No matter where you find yourself today, I believe that you can achieve a healthy body for life. The first place to begin is to evaluate where you are now. Your body will not change if you wallow in regret or remorse or continue to defend yourself with excuses.

Begin by asking yourself certain questions that move you toward a positive, healthy fitness future, rather than focus on your failures of the past.

- Do you have a family history of weight problems? Explain.
- Do you have certain genetic traits that cannot be changed by improving your eating or exercise habits? (i.e. height, bust size, bone size, shoe size, etc.)
- Have you consulted a physician recently who has given you an estimate of what your average weight should be for your age and height? If so, what is it? If not, why not?
- Can you name any eating habits that undermine your ability to eat moderately and healthy? (i.e. binge eating, eating in secret, skipping meals, excessive sugar or fatty-food cravings, etc.)
- Do you currently follow a regular exercise program? Describe.
- Have you ever followed an effective exercise plan? If so, describe. If not, explain why not.

These are just preliminary questions, but they can begin to help you identify and evaluate immediate physical changes that you can make today to improve your health.

Next, you must confront any unrealistic expectations or misconceptions that you have about achieving a healthy body.

An important aspect of the American life, especially emphasized in the media, focuses on having a perfect body. We strive so desperately to become like the lean, muscular, shapely models that are epitomized in our culture. We begin to believe that the bodies we are born with are not good enough. We have become a society where corrective, cosmetic surgery is no longer reserved for those over sixty, but is demanded by those in their teens and twenties.

As we continuously buy into the newest miracle method for weight loss, Americans have made an industry out of dieting that is worth billions of dollars. And even though there are more exercise gimmicks, and thousands of low-fat and non-fat foods on the market than ever before in history, government studies have found that Americans are fatter now than thirty years ago!

Whether fad dieting or plastic surgery, Americans have resorted to any means available—*other than disciplined eating and exercise habits*—to change their outward appearance.

Tend to Body Basics

There is a natural way to achieve a healthy, though perhaps not perfect, body.

You must determine to . . .

Accept your inherited traits.
Design and follow a lifelong plan for eating right and exercising regularly.

At a recent class on nutrition that I took at the renowned Cooper Institute in Dallas, Texas, it was suggested that individuals should not focus on an "ideal weight" but follow the guidelines for weight management set by the American Dietetics Association:

> The determination of ideal body weight is a very challenging question and one that is very commonly asked. Because it is impossible to establish a specific "ideal" body weight for all individuals, the American Dietetics Association proposed guidelines that do not attempt to pinpoint a specific value. They suggest that an ideal body weight would satisfy the following criteria:
>
> • Weight should not be too high to impair health
> • Weight should be low enough to permit physical activity
> • Weight should be maintained on a healthy diet
> • Weight should be acceptable to a person's self-esteem.

These guidelines are very general and perhaps fail to motivate the millions of us in the pursuit of healthy bodies because we are looking for daily, practical, and specific suggestions that will change our lives.

Rather than take the time to develop or exercise the discipline to follow a daily plan, the majority of us are prone to try fad diets, yo-yo dieting, or whatever is the current and quickest method to achieve weight loss.

In the Cooper Institute literature, we were given repeated resources that discounted and disproved the claims of the quick and easy diet solutions. We were strongly urged to avoid extreme or fad diets, not only because they don't work, but there is growing research that shows yo-yo dieting actually can keep the body from losing weight.

The most interesting thought that the Cooper Institute for Aerobics Research explored during the three-day Nutrition Specialty Certification for Providing Dietary Guidance was the simple fact that 3,500 calories = 1 pound. They stated that if you eat 3,500 *more* calories per year than your body requires, you will gain one pound each year. This little bit of information was not something I hadn't heard before, but when you consider that many of us eat an extra 3,500 calories each week or each month, you can quickly put into perspective how easy it is to gain weight! In other words, if what goes into your mouth exceeds your body's need for fuel, hydration, insulation, and cell restoration, this excess will be stored as extra weight, most likely in the form of fat. Only a practical, well-designed, daily plan could begin to help an individual monitor how to keep from gaining unwanted pounds.

Eating Right and Exercising Regularly As a Lifestyle

In each area of my life, I have identified two basic activities that I journal about on a daily basis. Each of the 8 Daily To Do's are simple and practical, and, if followed, the four balanced life areas will work together to bring balance into your entire life.

In the physical area, I believe that only a daily plan of eating right and exercising regularly can effectively maintain a lifelong approach to staying healthy and fit.

Although not quick or easy, the formula for planning an effective weight-loss program for any person of any age or weight-loss goal must be:

- **Realistic:** Weight gain occurs over a period of time. Unfortunately, it will also take time to come off. Small, daily goals will allow you to achieve long-term effects.

Food Guide Pyramid

A Guide to Daily Food Choices

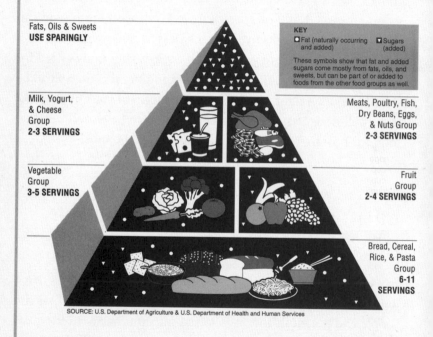

Fats, Oils & Sweets
USE SPARINGLY

KEY
□ Fat (naturally occurring and added)   ▼ Sugars (added)

These symbols show that fat and added sugars come mostly from fats, oils, and sweets, but can be part of or added to foods from the other food groups as well.

Milk, Yogurt, & Cheese Group
2-3 SERVINGS

Meats, Poultry, Fish, Dry Beans, Eggs, & Nuts Group
2-3 SERVINGS

Vegetable Group
3-5 SERVINGS

Fruit Group
2-4 SERVINGS

Bread, Cereal, Rice, & Pasta Group
6-11 SERVINGS

SOURCE: U.S. Department of Agriculture & U.S. Department of Health and Human Services

Use the Food Guide Pyramid to help you eat better every day . . . the Dietary Guidelines way. Start with plenty of Breads, Cereals, Rice, and Pasta; Vegetables; and Fruits. Add two to three servings from the Milk group and two to three servings from the Meat group.

Each of these food groups provides some, but not all, of the nutrients you need. No one food group is more important than another—for good health you need them all. Go easy on Fats, Oils, and Sweets, the foods in the small tip of the Pyramid.

To order a copy of "The Food Guide Pyramid" booklet, send a $1.00 check or money order made out to the Superintendent of Documents to: Consumer Information Center, Department 159-Y, Pueblo, Colorado 81009.

U.S. Department of Agriculture, Human Nutrition Information Service, August 1992, Leaflet No. 572

How to Use the Daily Food Guide

What counts as one serving?

Breads, Cereals, Rice, and Pasta
1 slice of bread
1/2 cup of cooked rice or pasta
1/2 cup of cooked cereal
1 ounce of ready-to-eat cereal

Vegetables
1/2 cup of chopped raw or cooked vegetables
1 cup of leafy raw vegetables
3/4 cup of vegetable juice

Fruits
1 piece of fruit or melon wedge
3/4 cup of juice
1/2 cup of canned fruit
1/4 cup of dried fruit

Milk, Yogurt, and Cheese
1 cup of milk or yogurt
1-1/2 to 2 ounces of cheese

Meat, Poultry, Fish, Dry Beans, Eggs, and Nuts
2-1/2 to 3 ounces of cooked lean meat, poultry, or fish
Count 1/2 cup of cooked beans, or 1 egg, or 2 tablespoons of peanut butter as 1 ounce of lean meat (about 1/3 serving)

Fats, Oils, and Sweets
LIMIT CALORIES FROM THESE especially if you need to lose weight

The amount you eat may be more than one serving. For example, a dinner portion of spaghetti would count as two or three servings of pasta.

How many servings do you need each day?

	Women & some older adults	Children, teen girls, active women, most men	Teen boys & active men
Calorie level*	about 1,600	about 2,200	about 2,800
Bread group	6	9	11
Vegetable group	3	4	5
Fruit group	2	3	4
Milk group	**2–3	**2–3	**2–3
Meat group	2, for a total of 5 ounces	2, for a total of 6 ounces	3, for a total of 7 ounces

*These are the calorie levels if you choose lowfat, lean foods from the 5 major food groups and use foods from the fats, oils, and sweets group sparingly.

**Women who are pregnant or breastfeeding, teenagers, and young adults to age 24 need 3 servings.

A Closer Look at Fat and Added Sugars

The small tip of the Pyramid shows fats, oils, and sweets. These are foods such as salad dressings, cream, butter, margarine, sugars, soft drinks, candies, and sweet desserts. Alcoholic beverages are also part of this group. These foods provide calories but few vitamins and minerals. Most people should go easy on foods from this group.

 Some fat or sugar symbols are shown in the other food groups. That's to remind you that some foods in these groups can also be high in fat and added sugars, such as cheese or ice cream from the milk group, or french fries from the vegetable group. When choosing foods for a healthful diet, consider the fat and added sugars in your choices from all the food groups, not just fats, oils, and sweets from the Pyramid tip.

- **Moderate:** Changes that are extreme or unnatural, inconvenient or impractical will rarely become habits. Changes made in increments or at a manageable pace are more likely to become lifestyle habits.
- **Consistent:** Scheduling your meals one day ahead and your workouts one week in advance—on a calendar—will allow alternate plans to be made when inevitable interruptions occur.
- **Supportive:** Having a workout partner, being a part of a support group, and informing your family and friends of your goals will give you the greatest chance for long-term success.

My purpose in attending the Cooper Institute was to increase my education and information about nutrition and exercise. I fully expected that we would be given a specific food and exercise plan to follow. Instead, we were each encouraged to develop an individualized eating and exercise plan based on our height, activity level, and desired weight.

They gave us the Food Guide Pyramid, which was not new information but simply the suggested, basic dietary guidelines for healthy eating. Using the Food Guide, we could see how many different food groups were intended to be part of our daily intake. Many of us had to increase in certain areas, and others of us realized that we exceeded suggested portions in certain food groups. The activity of looking at our food habits, then developing a healthy eating plan based on our activity level, gave us a sense of ownership for our choices and our health.

With the help of this chart, I encourage you to develop an eating plan that is right for you. With the consultation of a physician, and the support of a weight-loss group, you can determine what specific changes you can make that would improve your health—beginning today. These specialists can also help you real-istically determine how long it will take for you to lose your desired amount of weight, as well as give you suggestions for maintaining that weight loss for life.

The change your life Daily Journal

The change your life Daily Journal has played an essential part in helping me plan and achieve my eating and exercise goals on a daily basis. The simplicity of writing down what I plan to eat and when I plan to exercise has been the key to keeping me on a path of consistency from day to day, week to week, month to month, and eventually year to year.

Determining a daily course of action does not always mean that it will be achieved exactly as I have planned it, but it defi-nitely gives me a plan to follow. Should an inevitable interrup-tion occur, I have found it to be extremely important to be ready to implement an alternate eating or exercise plan on the same or next day. This flexibility allows me to change my plans without losing focus.

This past Saturday was one such day when the **Physical** page of **The change your life Daily Journal** helped me to adjust my plans without giving up my workout altogether.

During the week, I had noted three times when I would go to the gym. By Saturday, I had gotten to the gym two times for an indoor cycle class. My third (and final) workout of the week was scheduled for the Saturday 9:15 A.M. cycle class at the gym.

The evening before, our twenty-year-old son called to say that he and a friend would be staying at our house overnight and leaving for a water-ski trip early in the morning. He asked us to wake him up at 8 A.M.

After receiving his call, I took another look at my schedule and decided to get up a little earlier since he was coming home. I wanted to have my quiet time and make him a nice breakfast before leaving for the gym at 9:00 A.M.

By 8:30 A.M., it was obvious that the boys were not going to leave until mid-morning. I had a decision to make. If I wanted to enjoy a few more hours with my son, I was going to have to change the time of my scheduled workout. Between 8:30 A.M. and 9:00 A.M. on Saturday morning, I had to determine what I would do for my third workout. (I need to work out three times a week for approximately forty-five minutes to maintain my desired weight and eat the amount of food that I like to eat.)

My dilemma included two issues: there were no more indoor cycle classes scheduled at the gym on Saturday, except the 9:15 A.M. class, and because I had left my third workout of the week to the last day of the week, my alternate plan for working out would have to happen sometime during this day, which included other scheduled appointments.

I considered my options. First of all, I always prefer to work out with a partner or at a class taught by an instructor. Neither of these options was available to me at this late notice. So I decided to cycle at home on my indoor bike, using a home video. I knew this was going to take a lot of self-motivation, but I had purchased a home cycle so that if I had to exercise at home and alone, at least I would be able to do my current favorite workout.

Looking at the rest of my day's commitments showed me that the afternoon was my only option for working out. So in my journal, I rescheduled the time of my workout to 3:00 P.M. For extra support, I repeatedly told my husband throughout the day

date SAT

eat right

- · understand your own body type, genetics, metabolism, etc.
- · design a healthy, "plan ahead" eating plan that includes a balance of all the food groups in moderate portions
- · **record your daily intentions for meals and snacks below**
- · **review your progress and make daily adjustments**

breakfast	OATMEAL W/BERRIES, SKIM MILK
lunch	TURKEY SANDWICH ON RYE
dinner	SALMON, RICE, SALSA, BEANS
snacks	BAR, YOGURT W/ALMONDS

exercise regularly

- · determine what type of activity, where, when, how often and with whom you most like to exercise
- · develop a "week at a glance" exercise plan that includes a variety of 3 to 4 activities and has provision for alternate dates and times.

Detail your week plan; highlight today's plan.... what? when? where? with whom?

sun	mon	tue	wed	thur	fri	sat
						9:15 AM SPIN @ GYM

journal

Journal below about any temptations, circumstances or emotions—today—that might keep you from reaching your goals? (ex: vacation, celebrations, etc).

MOVIE CANDY

p
h
y
s
i
c
a
l

change
your
life
daily

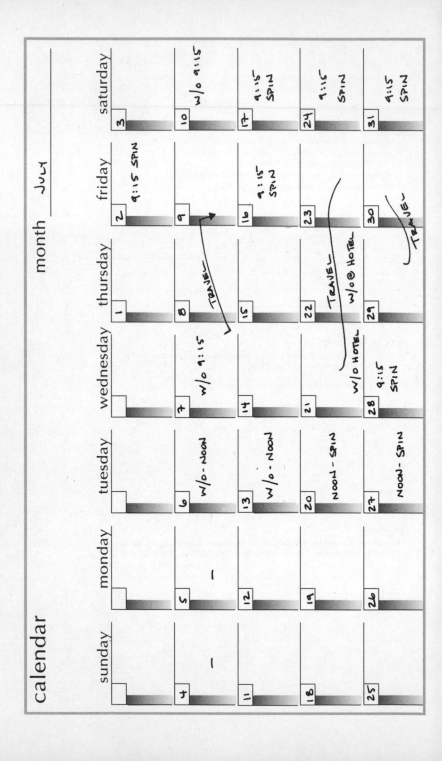

that I was planning to work out at home in the afternoon. It was 4:20 P.M. before I popped the video in the machine, but for thirty-five minutes with a fan blowing directly on my back, I met the challenge of exercising alone in eighty-five-degree weather. This was my least favorite workout of the week, *but* I thoroughly enjoyed the spontaneous hour that I had of eating, chatting, and packing clothes with my son.

In all honesty, if I had more days in my week, I would have preferred to switch my workout to another day. Squeezing your workouts into the last few days of the week or waiting until the last minute of the day can often lead to frustration and missed workouts. Scheduling three or four workouts over a seven-day period will give you more flexibility for finding alternate times to exercise.

The power of your written plan—as you journal and fill in a daily calendar—will give you an incredible amount of short-term success that will turn into months and years of consistency. I believe that your ability to achieve a healthy body will not be found in the complexity of the plan, but in the daily appointment that you have with yourself to chart how you will eat right and exercise regularly today and this week. Although your original plan may need to change, the goal of eating right and exercising regularly will never have to be compromised.

With any new eating or exercise program, it is important to consult a physician who can advise you of any restrictions that you should consider, based on your personal medical and genetic history or food allergies.

To find personal success and balance in this area of your life, you truly do owe it to yourself to further your physical education because *your* body is unique. As you will discover, there are three things you can count on:

- Your body will respond differently than someone else's to the same eating and exercise regimen.
- Don't underestimate the power of knowledge and truth to empower you to immediately change an old habit and establish a new, healthy habit.
- Keeping a written record of your healthy eating and exercise plan will give you accountability and momentum in achieving your fitness goals.

Eating Right

Recording on the **Physical** page of the journal what you *plan to eat*—one meal and one day at a time—can begin your pattern of improvement today!

Planning your meals one day at a time will empower you to fuel your body for maximum efficiency and energy and help you maintain your ideal weight and body shape, as well as relieve any temptation to eat poorly. Deciding in advance what "out-to-eat" options you have for certain meals will allow you to "pack a lunch" or call ahead and special order, if necessary.

On the **Physical** page of **The change your life Daily Journal** you are also given space to make notes of what possible pitfalls that you might face on a daily basis. A party, movie, or holiday can create obstacles as well as tempting traps such as gifts in the form of food, a candy counter at the theater, or appetizers and desserts that are displayed in unlimited quantity.

In my journal, I decide before I attend a dinner party if and how much I am going to eat of anything outside of my healthy eating plan. Most often, I find it easier to abstain from all of the delicacies, rather than limit myself to one or two treats. At the

date _____

eat right

- understand your own body type, genetics, metabolism, etc.
- design a healthy, "plan ahead" eating plan that includes a balance of all the food groups in moderate portions
- **record your daily intentions for meals and snacks below**
- **review your progress and make daily adjustments**

breakfast _____

lunch _____

dinner _____

snacks _____

exercise regularly

- determine what type of activity, where, when, how often and with whom you most like to exercise
- develop a "week at a glance" exercise plan that includes a variety of 3 to 4 activities and has provision for alternate dates and times.

Detail your week plan; highlight today's plan.... what? when? where? with whom?

sun	mon	tue	wed	thur	fri	sat

journal

Journal below about any temptations, circumstances or emotions—today— that might keep you from reaching your goals? (ex: vacation, celebrations, etc.)

_____

_____

_____

_____

_____

_____

physical

change
your
life
daily

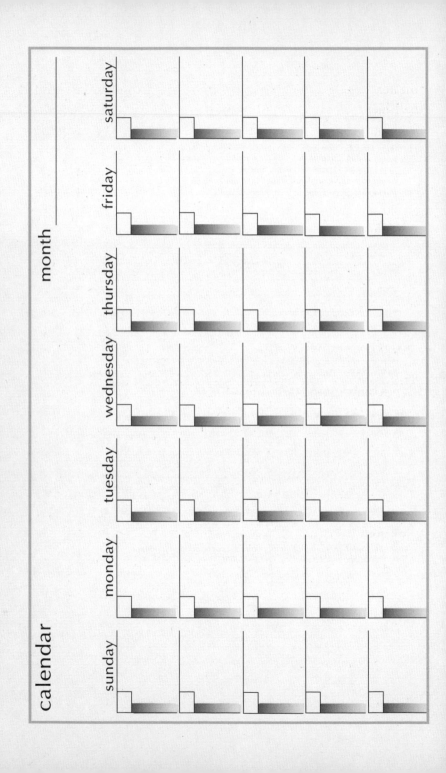

theater, I bring a food bar in my purse that I consider tasty but healthier than candy. And I rarely, if ever, drink calories. In addition, I try to make it a habit to eat only foods of which I know the caloric, fat, carbohydrate, and protein content. For example, if creamy, homemade foods are served that do not have identifiable contents, I steer away from them and enjoy more of the fresh vegetables and fruits that are available.

Other helpful hints for eating right include:

- Eating meats prepared without oil
- Asking for sauces on the side
- Eating vegetables that are steamed, rather than fried
- Using bread as a condiment, rather than a pre-meal appetizer
- Having salads *always* served with dressing on the side
- Using non-fat or low-fat milk for any milk recipes or drink supplements
- Eating until I am satisfied, not necessarily finishing everything on my plate
- Having occasional desserts that are lower in fat and calories, but primarily enjoying fresh fruit for dessert
- Eating half of a dessert; planning ahead to split one with someone at the meal
- Eating non-fat frozen yogurt as a dessert
- Avoiding fried foods
- Knowing how many calories are found in a certain portion of food
- Eating smaller portions at every meal

Exercise Regularly . . . Forever!

People often ask me if I exercise seven days a week. They seem amazed when I tell them that, due to my heavy travel schedule, I only work out three to four times a week for thirty-five to forty minutes each time. I have found that a realistic, manageable approach to exercise is to look at the seven days of each week and determine which three or four days I can plan workouts.

Planning your workouts *one week in advance* is the best way to achieve workout momentum and success. In the planning stage, it is important to be realistic about your family priorities, budget, and work commitments. I encourage you to be flexible and have an alternate set of plans for unexpected but inevitable interruptions. Remember that all physical activity, not just organized fitness classes, burns calories, reduces stress, improves your cardiovascular system, and lowers your cholesterol.

Choose some of the activities from the list below and incorporate them into your week with family, friends, and even your pets.

- Jogging outdoors, on a treadmill, or with kids in their stroller
- Walking outdoors or on a treadmill
- Biking outdoors or on an indoor cycle with an instructor or video
- Lifting weights
- Aerobics, low or high impact
- Hiking
- Golfing (carrying clubs)
- Tennis
- Swimming
- Rowing indoors (machine) or on water

- Boxing
- Soccer
- Basketball
- In-line skating
- Gardening
- Housework
- Baby-sitting or caring for little children

Many of us have committed to exercise for a specific period of time to achieve a certain goal with the intention of "taking a break" when we hit our mark. As soon as we reach our desired weight or size, we expect to find that our problems are over, the hard work has been done, and the goal is forever achieved! That is fantasy, not reality.

Sporadic exercise is only a temporary solution that will not produce permanent results. If you permanently desire to improve your cardiovascular fitness, burn calories, relieve stress, reduce inches and weight, change your body shape, and increase your energy, exercise must be a regular, weekly habit for your entire life.

The Surgeon General along with hundreds of fitness professionals suggest that in order to see changes in your body, or to maintain weight loss, you need to exercise three to five times each week for at least thirty minutes per workout session.

You don't need to be an expert in anatomy or physiology to observe that regular exercise makes a difference in your body weight and shape, as well as in your stress level and cardiovascular fitness. You only need to exercise regularly to validate the physical changes.

For me, the question has never been, "Does exercise work?" but rather, "How can I get myself to exercise?" *My* fitness program has to be fun, and include either companions or music. Whether I ride a mountain bike outdoors with a friend or go to the gym for a step or indoor cycle class, I have discovered which workouts keep me returning for more. Everyone is different! One of my friends wants her workout to be challenging rather than fun. (Can you imagine that? She rowed one million meters last year!) The key to *your* individual success will be to design and follow a fitness program that fits *your* personality, budget, lifestyle, and priorities.

Overall Physical Fitness

Being overweight, obsessed with weight, or out-of-control with your eating and exercise habits can cause mental, emotional, physical, and spiritual upheaval and imbalance in your life. Your eating and exercise patterns affect how you feel about and act toward yourself and others. For example, when you are unhappy with your appearance, you might become envious of another's body. Spiritually, your physical imbalance will affect your levels of peace and contentment, especially if you are constantly comparing yourself and competing with others. And mentally, if you do not help your body relieve stress with exercise, you become lethargic, irritable, and unproductive.

Eating Right and **Exercising Regularly** will benefit every area of your life:

PHYSICALLY

- Burns calories and fat
- Changes our body shape
- Reduces cholesterol levels
- Improves cardiovascular fitness
- Increases energy

- Builds muscle memory
- Enhances appearance

EMOTIONALLY

- Decreases stress
- Improves our attitude
- Relieves anxiety
- Can be an opportunity to develop new relationships
- Increases self-esteem and sense of satisfaction

SPIRITUALLY

- Builds character, patience, and persistence
- Promotes inner peace and contentment

MENTALLY

- Forces mind to clear out
- Develops discipline
- Promotes mind-over-body toughness (willpower)

Many of us adopted the principle of eating right and exercising regularly *only* after attempting to follow one or many faddish exercise or diet schemes. We have struggled repeatedly to discover the delicate balance between food consumption and physical exertion. The truth is that the process of eating right and exercising regularly is a lifelong pursuit that will continually need reevaluation and adjustment with each age and stage in our lives.

Remember, as you age, your body slows down. With each decade, you need to eat a little less and exercise a little more. Always take into consideration what activities you like and are available within your area and budget as you develop your daily written action plan.

By recording—in a journal—your daily action plan to eat right and exercise regularly, you will develop lifelong habits that can be maintained—with variety and adjustment—throughout your entire life. Of course, all of these decisions will revolve around your particular conditions of life. Your priorities will help determine how often, long, and what type of exercise is right for you.

As millions of Americans can attest, simply achieving your physical fitness goals will never provide you with ultimate contentment and meaning in life. When you tend to body basics by **Eating Right** and **Exercising Regularly** you bring balance into the physical area of your life and are better able to pursue healing in your relationships, connect with God, and fulfill your life purpose with momentum and confidence.

Heal and Be Healed (Emotional)

Forgive
Give

BENEFIT: *Emotional healing generates relationship healing.*

TRUTH: *Forgiving and giving, when practiced on a daily basis, are two practical activities that can stimulate amends, instigate reunions, and restore what was once wounded, lost, or stolen.*

What do you do when you find yourself in a broken or wounded relationship or you have become isolated from others and God? If you are like me, then your first reaction will be to blame others or make excuses. But those responses never result in healed relationships or break the cycle of unhealthy emotional reactions.

You and I are involved daily in significant and surface relationships that will flourish or fade based on our level of emotional health. And our interactions with others can act as a barometer for our emotional health. How you feel and think on any given day will determine how well you get along with others. I know that how I relate to my husband, son, or mother indicates whether or not I am in a healthy emotional place. I believe that if my relationships are healthy, it is a very good indicator that my emotions are healthy.

That healthy emotional place is something that I desire. It doesn't mean that I have to forgo my feelings or deny them. It means that I have had to learn to manage my emotions by practicing two daily principles for emotional healthy living—**Forgiving** and **Giving.** In the past year, I have had the opportunity to break a very destructive cycle from my past.

It Began When I Was
a Teenager . . .

My mom and I have always had a very robust style of interaction. We are both strong-willed, forceful with our emotions, and desire to be in control whenever possible.

By the time I was a teenager, my mother and I developed a loud, demeaning, and hostile pattern of communication that repeatedly ended in tension, power struggles, sharp words, or critical comments. I was unafraid to be brutally honest and verbal with my feelings, whereas my siblings were usually compliant, speaking to our parents with respect.

By the time I had turned twenty-one, married, and had a child, my relationship with my mother became less hostile, but I did not want to spend time with her. She was happy about my sobriety, spirituality, and maturity, but our core personalities still clashed whenever we were in the same room for very long.

In 1985, I moved to California, and our relationship maintained a kinder civility because we had fewer opportunities to spend extended periods of time together.

When I became an author and began to make public speaking appearances, I spoke freely about my volatile teenage years. In telling my story, I almost prided myself in painting a vivid picture with detailed descriptions of how the mixture of alcohol and anger had affected every aspect of my life—past and present. I thought that my transparent story was an eye-opening description that could serve as a warning to other families who were living in this manner.

In 1994, I returned home to Cleveland to share my story in front of forty thousand people. My entire extended family and numerous friends were planning to come to hear me speak. Just before we got in the car to drive downtown to the Cleveland Municipal Stadium, my mother took me aside and expressed her concerns. Through tears, she shared that she was afraid that I was going to humiliate her and my father with the details of our family's past.

At first I was defensive. I didn't want to be told what to do or how to tell my story. But my mother's honesty shed new light on the situation. It is one thing to give every sordid detail of *your* life in public; it is another thing to give the details of another person's life without their approval or consent.

Although I thought I had been helping others with my story, in the process I had been exposing and wounding my mother and father every time I spoke!

In that brief exchange, I realized that I had been trying to hurt my mother for years. I had placed the entire blame for the many years of emotional upheaval and insecurity that I felt as a teenager on her, even though it was my dad who had been the alcoholic. The reality of our family life between the '50s and '70s was that both of my parents struggled with anger and alcohol. Most of the time my mother was trying to keep our finances afloat, food on the table, and even uphold a "happy family" image in our community. I was the youngest child, the most rebellious, and by the time I was thirteen, emotional survival was my only goal. It was also my mother's goal. I realized that I was still trying to punish her for not protecting me from that atmosphere.

Up until that moment, I would have told you that I had forgiven my parents for those unhappy years. My willingness to give every audience a blow-by-blow description of how terrible my life was as a teenager had given me some odd form of vindication, a sweet revenge.

It wasn't until my mother confronted me that I finally understood that I had been trying to get even with my parents, to hurt them back.

Before the event, I promised my mother that, from that day on, I would not describe our relationship and family life in the way in which I had been freely exposing and condemning them for years. I told her that I would only give the details about *my* past, rather than exploit my parents' lives in public.

That weekend, I became aware of my desire to hurt my parents, but I didn't really ask them to forgive me. In my heart, I continued to look at this situation as their fault or problem and I would simply comply with their request for privacy by not telling their part of the story. That safe, almost self-righteous, approach to solving this problem allowed me to discount my actions, but it ultimately kept me from healing for four more years.

As months, and then years went by, I kept my word and shared my story in such a way as to protect the reputation of my parents. But I still did not want to spend any length of time with them. (This should have been a red flag to alert me of my unforgiveness, but a wounded spirit puts up a great defense.) I held them at arm's length, not exhibiting a warm, child-like affection when I was with them. Instead, I determined how long I would visit them on the holidays or how long they could come to my house and stay. I did not view this coldness as unforgiveness, but as a boundary I had put in place to protect me from experiencing any more emotional pain.

One night, I attended a small group meeting where many women shared deep pain from their past. But rather than wallow in self-pity, at the meeting's end, we were each encouraged to apologize in writing to someone whom *we* had hurt.

The following morning as a matter of habit, I turned to the **Forgive** section on the **Emotional** page of **The change your life Daily Journal.** The thought-provoking question on that page each day asks, "Is there anyone you need to ask to forgive you for hurting them?" (Because I daily answer this question, current circumstances quickly pop into my mind. It is the deeper hurts, issues, and past pain that can stay buried, if we let them.) Having nothing current to journal about, I reflected on the previous night's group meeting. My mother came to mind.

I reflected back to the incident in 1994. Further journaling revealed how I had never humbly and sincerely asked my parents to forgive me for how I had hurt them by exposing the details of my childhood in my books and at my lectures. I could not recall actually asking my parents for forgiveness.

It was during that journal experience that a new thought crossed my mind. My unforgiveness was the reason I kept an emotional distance from my parents, especially my mother. Could I have been holding back healing in our relationship because of my stubborn reluctance to let go of a painful, long ago, never-to-be-repeated memory?

I took extra time during my journal appointment to write a letter to my mother. In my letter, I told her how sorry I was for wanting to hurt her and for publicly humiliating her during my many speeches and in books. I told her I loved her and I truly did want to have a loving relationship with her. I humbly asked her to forgive me. Then, I let the letter sit on the kitchen table for a few days. There was still a tiny bit of reservation within me, afraid that reopening this situation might create a whole new set of problems or release undue emotional pain. By the end of the week, I threw the letter away, thinking that it had served the purpose of revealing my unwillingness to heal my relationship with my mother.

On Saturday, I got out of bed very early and called my mother in Cleveland. She answered the phone, delighted to hear my voice. But she was surprised to hear from me. She asked, "Why did you call, Becky?"

I replied, "I don't know."

She said, "You won't believe this. I was just listening to an old tape of your story, you know, the way you told it before the Cleveland event. It is one of the times when you shared how terrible we were as parents. It made me cry."

"I do know why I called," I whispered quietly.

I told her about my journal experience, and the letter that I had written to her but, for some reason, hadn't sent.

Then I apologized—in depth—for trying to hurt her, for being unforgiving, and for exposing so much of her life to other people without her permission. I asked her to forgive me.

In her seventy-seven-year-old Cleveland way, she exclaimed, "It's a miracle!" My mother was so touched by my phone call and apology that she could barely contain her emotions. We had lived with a barrier between us for most of our adult lives. I had not let her over or through the barrier until this moment. When I asked her to forgive me, she knew that I had knocked down the wall between us and she was finally free from my bitterness and anger.

There was a very real sense between us that we were in the middle of an emotionally healing experience. She was released from my unforgiveness. She was deeply touched. She was healed emotionally.

Then came an even more unexpected healing.

She said, "Becky, I've always felt terrible about how unhappy your teenage years were at home. Your dad and I were struggling to survive financially, and in other ways. I am ashamed for how Dad and I hurt you when you were a child. I never wanted my friends to think that our lives were so out of control. And we did not have personal relationships with God then, either. Our priorities were so confused. I am so sorry for any hurt and pain that I have caused you. *Will you forgive me?*"

I was speechless. I had waited twenty-two years to hear my mother say those words. At various times during those years, I had tried to manipulate and orchestrate ways to get her to apologize to me, validating my pain. But those words never came.

In my own forty-three-year-old Californian way, I replied, "It's a miracle!"

Immediately, a favorite verse that I had previously memorized came to mind, "Confess your sins to one another so that *you* may be healed."

My confession and admission resulted not only in my mother's healed emotions, but I was touched and healed when she asked me to forgive her. Little did I know how important this conversation would later become, or how it would be the beginning of a new, loving, strong, even fun relationship with my mother.

The following spring, I happened to mention to my mother that my neighbor's mother and mother-in-law lived in a retirement community fifteen minutes from my house. I also mentioned that it had two golf courses within its gates. When she immediately asked if she could come look at the community for housing, I was quiet. This was not in the plan. The plan had always been that my mother, when she was ready, would leave Cleveland and move to Northern California where my older sister lived. My mom and sister have always gotten along beautifully. (And just for the record, there are over two hundred baby pictures of my sister and only five of me!) Not once had the thought crossed my mind of my mother living in Southern California near me. I had never even considered it an option.

But she was persistent. She called me once a week to ask how soon she could visit and if I would please find out the name of my neighbor's realtor.

When I told my husband what my mother and I had been discussing, he said, "Becky, what were you thinking? You and your mother have never gotten along very well when you lived near each other."

I, too, was uncertain how things would work out if my mother moved close to me. What if we still struggled? What if she wanted to spend too much time with me? I didn't want to revert to our old relationship. Living miles apart had been safer.

It was too late to change the momentum. I was going to have the opportunity to see if our relationship had been truly healed because she had booked a flight to arrive in California on May 21! I called my neighbor and arranged for her realtor to meet with us on May 22.

On the evening of May 21, I returned home from picking my mom up at the airport to a call left on my answering machine. The realtor, whom I had never met but who had been very highly recommended to us, was unable to meet with us. She was sending another realtor to show us property in the morning. The next message on the answering machine was the other realtor. She asked me to call her. I was resistant. I thought, "I don't know this other woman. We should just wait." I dialed her number and when she answered, I was somewhat cold toward her. I simply did not want to meet with a different realtor. But she proceeded to ask me specific questions regarding a place for my mother.

I sighed. Now we were going to have to deal with my fears. My mother was an interior decorator. She was very picky. She was not going to go for shag carpet, purple paint, inappropriate window coverings, poor lighting, or anything else aesthetically unpleasing to the eye.

When I finished giving all of the reasons I thought it was going to be impossible to find a perfect house for my mother, I added that my mom was from Cleveland. In Ohio, you could get a lot more for your money. With the money my mom would have to spend after she sold her home, I thought it would be very unlikely that we would find something suitable for her in her price range in California.

There was another issue. My mother had lived in her little three-bedroom home for over forty years. It was in a family neighborhood, had a well-manicured garden, and its interior and exterior were decorated like a current decorator's magazine. I just couldn't fathom how we were going to find a condominium to take the place of her home.

When I was finished whining, the realtor said, "You won't believe this, but I think I have just the place for your mother."

"What do you mean?" I asked.

"Without going into too much detail, a good friend of mine has asked that I list his condominium. I just got the listing tonight and have not yet had time to put the home into the multiple listing system. Therefore, no one knows that it is for sale. But, I will honestly tell you that as soon as it is listed, it will sell immediately," she said.

"Why is that?" I asked.

She came forward with the details. "The owner was an artist. It is a beautifully decorated condominium that overlooks a green belt, has wood blinds, new tile, special lighting fixtures, built-in cabinets, a loft, a bedroom, a guest room, and the asking price is near your budget."

My husband, mother, and I visited the condominium before noon the next day. In fact, we were in it only a few minutes when my mother had to walk outside because she was so overwhelmed with emotion. She was shocked that every room seemed designed to perfectly suit her taste and fit her furniture. Once outside, she began to cry. She said, "I could have never imagined that God would have such a perfect place for me."

Within twenty minutes, we put an offer on the condominium. Before the weekend was over, the deal was done!

Two weeks later, my mother returned to Cleveland and sold her home. She had all of her belongings—and car—moved to California in August, the very week that escrow closed on both homes.

Before she even moved here, I asked her if she wanted to work for me at my office. She had been hoping to find a small, fun job to give her a little extra income. Since the first week my mother lived in California, I have invited her to sleep at my house or work at the office at least once a week. We go to movies together, shop, enjoy her home-cooked meals, eat out, golf occasionally, and talk on the phone almost daily. We've taken out-of-state trips together, and thoroughly enjoy each other's company, ideas, and suggestions. My husband is amazed at how wonderfully we get along!

For most of my life, I have withheld love and forgiveness from my mother—until now. When I took the step of asking her to forgive me, we were both healed. I regret that I missed so many years of enjoying the blessing of being loved by my mother because of my own stubborn unforgiveness. *I had kept myself* from experiencing the healing that comes from reconciliation.

I now have a great respect and deep admiration for my mother. She is emotionally strong, very loving, athletic (golfs three days a week), talented, artistic, helpful, giving, and supportive. In fact, I want to be just like her!

Because I have experienced how wonderful it is to have a great relationship with someone I have struggled with in the past, I want everyone to have the same opportunity. I am confident that if you will begin to journal every day with the goal of finding emotional and relationship healing, you will find the way to reconciliation. But you might have to take the first step and offer a sincere apology or make amends with anyone whom you have hurt, no matter if they have previously hurt you.

Is It Time for You to Heal?

Emotional healing is a process that takes time, but if you will **Forgive** and **Give** on a daily basis, I believe that you will begin to experience healing within yourself *and* your relationships. These two specific activities will bring relief, hope, healing, reconciliation, freedom, and forgiveness to everyone—whether you are relatively well adjusted or severely wounded.

I often refer to **Forgiving** and **Giving** as *"the Twelve Steps in two steps!"* If you've not studied the Twelve Steps in great detail, they essentially encompass two themes. The first eleven steps suggest that the path to wholeness and healing begins when you ask God and others to forgive you, and continues when you offer to forgive others. The Twelfth Step suggests that the outward sign of inner healing and growth is expressed through the love and help you give to others—as a response to the love and help that you have received.

You can begin to heal your emotions and relationships by reaching into your soul to discover when you have been hurt, what continues to hurt you, and why. Asking and answering questions like the ones listed below is the awareness step that can be a starting place for inner healing. I also want to encourage you to take an action step and journal about any of the thoughts, issues, conflicts, fears, or unresolved issues that come to mind as your read through and answer these questions.

- Why do I get so angry?
- Why do I feel so sad?
- Why do I overreact?
- What do those closest to me observe about me?
- Who do I want to avoid? Why?
- Who do I constantly take advantage of?
- Why am I so selfish?
- What am I afraid to lose?
- Why do I sabotage certain relationships?
- What do I want that I can't have?
- How have I hurt someone in the same way someone has hurt me?
- Who have I hurt that deserves an apology from me?
- Who do I fear?
- What am I hiding about?
- Am I lying to myself or to another about anything?

On the **Emotional** page of **The change your life Daily Journal,** you are given journal space to **Forgive** and **Give** on a daily basis. If you are creating your own journal, this page can be a blank piece of paper that you divide in half. The top half is the place to journal about your day's forgiveness issues, and the bottom half of the page is the place to make a record of how you can daily be a giving person.

This is not meant to be just another intellectual exercise. It is an activity that is designed to intentionally move you toward reconciling yourself to others and to God—on a daily basis. Through the practical effort of honest communication *and* by giving of your time, talents, and money to those around you, you will daily begin to experience healing and change.

FORGIVE

Each day in the **Forgive** section of **The change your life Daily Journal,** you are asked to "let go of," "forgive," or "release" someone or something through the journaling experience. It is not always possible or necessary to immediately resolve every situation—especially if it requires a response from someone else. But you can begin *your* healing process by asking God to help you identify both anyone whom you might have hurt or your own unforgiving feelings toward someone who has hurt you.

It is a biblical principle that if you withhold forgiveness from another, it will keep you from experiencing emotional health. In the New Testament Gospel of Matthew, Jesus talked about forgiveness. He was very direct. He said, "If you forgive those who sin against you, your heavenly Father will forgive you. But if you refuse to forgive others, your Father will not forgive your sins" (NLT, Mt 6:14). Later, when one of his disciples asked how many

date _____

e

m

o

t

i

o

n

a

l

forgive

To experience emotional balance on a daily basis, allow one or more of the below questions to prompt you to journal about the relationships in your life that need to heal and be healed.

Today, I know I need to ask _____ **to forgive me.**

I need to forgive myself for _____

I need to forgive _____ **for** _____

And I ask God to forgive me for _____

_____

_____

_____

_____

_____

_____

What additional step(s) can I take to complete the healing that I have just journaled about in the above space? (ex: a phone call, letter, apology, etc.)

_____

_____

_____

_____

give

The gift of time, money, resources, or talent to an organization or person is both a powerful and practical way to help others.
What need comes to my mind—today—that I can find and fill and/or what person or organization needs a specific source of comfort or encouragement that I can give?

_____

_____

_____

_____

_____

_____

change

your

life

daily

times he should forgive when someone sinned against him, Jesus responded, "I tell you, not seven times but seventy-seven times!" (NIV, Mt 18:22). Jesus taught forgiveness as a non-negotiable principle for living, not an option.

In the Gospel of Mark, Jesus reiterated to his followers that forgiving others is essential if we want to receive forgiveness from God, as well as to receive answers to our prayers. He stated, "And when you stand praying, if you hold anything against anyone, forgive him, so that your Father in heaven may forgive your sins" (NIV, Mark 11:25).

I believe that if you truly desire to bring the emotional area of your life into balance, you must make it a lifestyle habit to forgive others and ask God to forgive you *on a daily basis.* As you are honest about your own imperfections, you will become less judgmental and critical of others. As you extend forgiveness, you will react and respond to others with humility and kindness, rather than with selfishness or anger. Forgiveness is the catalyst that causes relationships to begin to heal.

Forgiving others and asking God to forgive you opens the path to a clean, clear connection with God. It releases happiness within your spirit and soul. You are free to smile and relax and enjoy others when you do not hold grudges or withhold love.

Many people write to me with their stories of personal healing as a result of forgiving someone who had hurt them. One woman shared how the first day that she journaled in the **Forgive** section, a friend of hers immediately came to mind because they hadn't spoken for over nine months. Because she was prompted to ask herself specific questions about unresolved issues and relationships in her life, she took the opportunity to journal about the incident that had caused her and her friend to stop talking. As she journaled, she could see that they were both at fault and that there was probably miscommunication on both sides. That insight caused her to look at the situation from a different perspective. She asked God to forgive her, and then she bravely called her estranged friend. She began the conversation with an apology. The result? Her friend apologized as well. They immediately rekindled their relationship.

The **Forgive** section has the ability to help you uncover and gently sift through many of your unresolved issues, broken relationships, and unsettling anxieties. You will also find that journaling on the **Emotional** page will reveal if your eating patterns are influenced by unresolved anger and unforgiveness. When you are not at peace with yourself and others, you may turn to food to comfort or hide your feelings. You might even find that journaling can be a replacement for binge eating or drinking.

As you heal emotionally, you will begin to focus less on yourself and more on others, even looking for ways to reach out and make a difference in the lives of others.

GIVE

There is and will always be someone who has less than you do, needs something that you have, or could be encouraged or helped by your assistance, generosity, care, concern, comment, or helping hand. The practice of giving to others on a daily basis has the potential to change not only the recipient, but also the giver. But exerting the extra effort, even going beyond what is expected of us, is the exception rather than the rule for most of us.

Ruth Peale, wife of Norman Vincent Peale, said, "Find a need and fill it." This statement has become a mantra for many organizations. How wonderful—and healing—it would be if it were the daily passion of every individual.

Since I began to journal on a regular basis in the **Give** section of **The change your life Daily Journal,** I have been amazed at how many ways I have been challenged to help another or step outside of my comfort zone to really make a difference in someone's life. This section of the journal has opened my eyes to see how often I lean more toward being selfish than being selfless.

One such occasion occurred recently on a Sunday morning. As I often do, I woke up early and had my journal appointment with God. In the **Give** section of **The change your life Daily Journal,** I wrote down the words "help out in the nursery department at church." Hmm. I had never worked in the nursery before. I had spent years in Sunday morning classes with teenagers, but never with infants or toddlers.

I knew there was a need for volunteers because our church was full of young families. Just as we were getting ready for church, I mentioned the idea to Roger. He said, "If you are going to work in the nursery, then why are you wearing a dress?" I hadn't considered the fact that babies who can't walk play on the floor. So I ran upstairs, changed into pants, and found Roger waiting at the front door for me—in blue jeans!

I said, "Why are *you* dressed so casually for church?"

He replied nonchalantly, "Because we're going to work in the nursery."

What a great guy! As we drove to church, I reflected on how cool I thought we were to help out at a nursery when our son was almost twenty years old. I fantasized about the sweet little babies who just wanted to be held.

When we entered the nursery room, it was very noisy. Shouting over the little voices, I asked if any moms would like to attend the first service. Because we were a well-known couple in the church, the security requirements were waived, and we immediately filled two helper spots.

Rog was sent off to be with the toddlers. Because the building we rented had few recreational facilities, he proceeded to be a bas-

ketball hoop for 1½ hours. I had the sheer delight of changing dia-
pers, picking up smashed Cheerios from the floor (and feeding them
to the hungriest children), while rubbing the bumps and bruises
that the babies acquired during crashes and pileups on my watch.

It was hard work. I never realized how difficult it was to coor-
dinate the squirming bodies of ten infants, even with the help of
four adults in the room! When I next saw Rog, his few bald hairs
were sticking straight up in the air and his shirt tail had been
yanked outside of his pants.

We were exhausted after the short time with the kiddies and
headed right home without hearing a sermon or singing a song. I
thought, "That's enough nursery for me this year!"

Ironically, the following Sunday, our young pastor made a plea.
He said, "If you have volunteered to do something, but you didn't
really like it, please give it at least three tries before you give up. We
need all the help we can get, especially with the younger children."

I knew this meant that I would have to return to the nursery.
And even though being with babies is not my favorite way to give
of myself, I felt good about giving a young mom an opportunity
to be encouraged spiritually and sit with her husband at church.

It is often while journaling in the **Give** section of my journal
that I can clearly see my selfish, lazy side. In the process, I uncover
my stubbornness, or unwillingness to give of myself, and I am
faced with an opportunity to change.

While journaling this past January 1, I absolutely knew what
I should write down in the **Give** section of the **Emotional** page of
The change your life Daily Journal, but I was reluctant. The act
of writing down my intention to give something specific to someone doesn't always immediately translate into a completed task,
but it does get my mind and heart moving in the right direction,
until my actions catch up.

I have been married over twenty-one years. I have given—at

most—three back rubs to my husband during the first twenty-one years of marriage, although he would have been happy to receive regular, daily back rubs. Somehow, I got out of giving back rubs (because I am lazy) by claiming that my arms and fingers become too fatigued within the first few seconds. As a result of my disinterest and lack of skill, Roger's request for massages faded early in our marriage. As an added precaution, I was careful never to ask for a back rub, thus indebting myself to return the favor. Twenty years quietly passed.

Then during the last few days of December, a friend sent me a Christmas gift—a "how to" massage video, complete with oil! The moment I opened the package, I had two strong impressions: how little I knew—or wanted to know—about giving a massage, and a question about where I could hide the video so my husband wouldn't see it.

A few days later, on January 1, I started journaling in a brand new **change your life Daily Journal.** It was a new year, a new month, a new day . . . I was excited!

With enthusiasm that comes from a fresh start, I recorded how I was going to **Eat Right** and **Exercise Regularly** on the **Physical** page, then I automatically turned to the **Emotional** journal page. I reflected deeply and wrote easily in the **Forgive** section. But when my eyes drifted below to the **Give** section on the same page, I had one relentless thought, "Give Roger a massage."

I tried to think of anything else to write down, but I could not. So, I wrote out my intentions but did not give myself a due date by which to give Roger a massage. By the evening of January 1, my husband began to complain of an aching back. I thought he had been reading my journal or had found the video, but then I remembered that we had gone bowling on New Year's Eve! The fifth game had apparently taken its toll on my aging, fifty-two-year-old husband.

I instinctively knew that a back rub or massage would be a nice, welcomed, helpful, kind, and healing gesture. But I could not get myself to say the words that would commit me to the activity. I remained selfishly silent and simmered with self-inflicted guilt.

Even my brother had a sense of Roger's discomfort and suggested that he get in the hot tub to relieve his aching back. He did—which temporarily alleviated his pain and my guilt for another day.

On January 2, I once again turned to the **Give** section of my journal—and again wrote down the good, kind, and thoughtful intention to give my husband a back massage. As the day wore on, I still could not get myself to mention the idea to him.

That evening, we headed off to the movies, a date night that we put on our calendar almost once a week. When we got to the ticket counter we were told that our movie choice was sold out, which is a rarity in a fifteen-theater city.

I couldn't stop the next thought: "If I was truly unselfish, I would offer to give Rog a massage. I could make a big deal of it, telling him how I had received an instructional massage video as a gift. I could offer to give him a technically correct massage for his aching back!" My mind bantered back and forth with this idea for at least two or three minutes, while Rog was meanwhile suggesting a variety of other date-night options.

Ultimately, motivated by my journal writing, my heart followed my desire to become less selfish and more giving. I blurted out, "If we go home, I could put on a massage video that I got as a Christmas gift. Perhaps a massage might bring some relief to your aching back? Would you like that?"

His response? He said *nothing,* but simply gave me the most surprised, starry-eyed, skeptical, and happy look that a husband could give his wife, then whisked me off to the parking lot! Of course, we immediately sped home. With a very willing attitude, I proceeded to open the shrink-wrapped video and oil, then laid out a large sheet on the floor for the massage.

Over and over, while journaling, I understand the emotional healing power that is released when I give. Although giving is almost always admired by those observing or receiving, it can often be inconvenient, hard, and costly for the giver. Whether it is time or money or a possession, the true value of the gift is relative to the giver. The very same action may cost one person more or less sacrifice than it will cost another person.

I am finding that the more costly something is for me to give, the deeper I have to dig inside of myself to exert true compassion, selflessness, sacrifice, and generosity. Those qualities not only build and refine my character but also bring me an immeasurable amount of emotional and relationship healing.

Within the safe confines of my journal, I have been able to confront my personality flaws, admit my anger and resentments, and forgive others.

The more willing I am to forgive and give, the quicker I have been able to turn from unhealthy addictions, resentments, obsessive eating, yelling, unforgiveness, self-centeredness in my marriage, procrastination, and other self-destructive behaviors. My journal is also the place where I have been honest enough with God and myself to realize that I have hurt others and need to ask them for their forgiveness.

The practical activity of journaling about how I can resolve my anger, forgive others, ask for forgiveness, as well as reach out to others has a direct and dramatic effect on my emotional health. The sooner I let go of something, confess my part in it, or gently confront an issue, the sooner a relationship is renewed and my emotional state is happy and healthy.

My mother, husband, and son are most often the first recipients of a positive journal experience. My coworkers, friends, and business acquaintances also receive my apologies more quickly because of this daily habit. I have found nothing more practical than these two daily activities to improve my relationships and bring healing to my emotions.

In the process of daily **Forgiving** and **Giving,** I not only receive healing for myself, and healing within my relationships, but I also have an opportunity to live in a new way and break cycles from my past. This part of my journal experience prepares my spirit for a transparent and honest conversation with the living, loving God.

SIX

Connect with God (Spiritual)

Talk to God
Listen to God

BENEFIT: *Connecting with God through a two-way conversation unleashes inner peace, reveals purpose for living, and develops a personal relationship with the living, loving God.*

TRUTH: *Journaling provides a practical method for talking to God. The Bible, God's written Word, is His voice to mankind. It provides a tangible response from God and eliminates an elusive pursuit of God.*

Without reservation, I can say that I made a radical but practical decision over fifteen years ago that has been the driving force behind my continual pursuit of change. When I determined to set aside one hour every day for the rest of my life to meet with God—through journaling—I had no idea how much clarity, focus, improvement, continued awareness, and courage it would give me.

Of course, this resolution came as a result of dissatisfaction, setbacks, and frustration—as have most of my dramatic and life-changing decisions. Tired of being indecisive, impulsive, and anxious, I wanted to change so many areas of my life that I concluded only God could help me.

I knew the drill. I would have to "let go," and relinquish control of my plans, and ask God to help me make decisions based on *His will and plan* for my life.

I knew from previous experience that a "once-a-year high" received at a convention or retreat was never going to maintain the level of intimate communication that I desired to have with God. I determined that the only way to find ultimate balance in every area of my life was to connect with God on a *daily* basis. It was a great idea, but I was going to have to find a practical method for achieving such a serious spiritual discipline.

Peter Marshall, former chaplain of the Senate, fondly spoke about his relationship with God in "sailor" vernacular. He said that it was during his daily conversations with God that he would "get his marching orders from the Captain." He believed that God divinely met with him each morning and that their appointment was not simply a matter of spiritual communion, but a place where he received his tactical assignments for fulfilling his purpose on earth.

That is what I was looking for—a method of communicating with God where I would talk to Him, pour my heart out and express my desires to Him, share my fears and concerns with Him, then receive His response.

Within days of making a decision to spend time with God *for one hour every day for the rest of my life,* a practical pattern unfolded which utilized resources that had always been available to me.

I designed my own simple method for having a two-way conversation with God. I imagined that Jesus was sitting with me at my kitchen table. On blank sheets of notebook paper, I would tell Him everything that was in my heart and on my mind that morning. I envisioned Him carefully listening to me, expecting Him to respond to me with direction, correction, and wise advice.

In order to hear God's voice, I knew that I didn't want to just close my eyes and grasp for a thought. I wanted something more tangible, so I made it a habit to open my Bible to a favorite chapter and read until I heard His voice. As I read the Bible each day, it seemed inevitable that one or two verses would relate to my situation or reveal an insight that was helpful to my previous written journal entries. I would receive the impression that God, Himself, was meeting with me.

My daily two-way conversations would subtly reveal if I was overly frustrated, anxious, angry, or trying to hide something. Almost immediately they began to impact and influence every area of my life—physically, emotionally, relationally, financially, and mentally.

First of all, I became aware that I wasn't always the same person in public that I was in private. I noticed that I frequently burst out in anger at my son, who was a toddler at the time. Even though I only did this at home, I knew I would be ashamed of myself if I behaved that way in public. It was during my conversations with God that I found myself saddened by my inability to control my anger with my son, especially as I had resented being yelled at as a child. But I also found that God did not reject me for my honesty. In fact, it was during those daily appointments that I would be inspired to change certain approaches, attitudes, and activities.

As I spent more time with God, other areas of weakness would "pop" into my mind. I began to tell God the truth about my feelings and thoughts. I was jealous of others who had more, looked better, and seemed smarter. These revelations were rather humiliating, but I knew God could help me to change.

And change I did. I will admit that change with God's help is not always comfortable, but it *is* transforming.

I have followed a simple pattern each day for over fifteen years. I talk to God in writing and then listen to God by reading the Bible.

I begin my conversation with God by telling Him that I love Him, I trust Him, and I believe in Him. I list the ways that I recognize His power and unchanging character in the world and in my life. I ask Him to guide my life. I use the Psalms, which are written prayers, as a pattern for expressing my love toward God.

Next, I have made it a daily routine to write out the 23rd and 24th verses from Psalm 139, "Search me, O God, and know my heart. Test me and know my anxious thoughts. See if there is any offensive way in me and lead me in the way that is everlasting." If I have had a disagreement with someone and have not been willing to or able to admit my part, or make an apology, these verses *always* bring to my mind any unresolved issues or hurting relationships in my life. They also give me specific situations to journal about in the **Emotional** section of **The change your life Daily Journal.** The Bible repeatedly mentions, and I have learned by experience, that a clean heart, pure motives, and a clear conscience are prerequisites for receiving answers to prayer.

Then, I talk to God about specific people I know who need His help. I often ask for His supernatural intervention for the sick, poor, addicted, spiritually lost, and strugglers. I also ask God to give me advice and direction on specific business or family decisions, purchases, and professional projects. I discuss my employee situations, husband's needs, son's safety, his friends and educational decisions, as well as my finances. I share all these concerns with God—in writing—every day.

I also write a thank-you note to God. I name the specific ways that I have seen His guidance and assistance in my life. Whether it is a timely phone call, an exciting and long-awaited personal or professional dream that becomes a reality, or a "no" that turns into a "yes," I thank God—in writing—for caring about the details of my life.

Connecting with God begins with talking to God. However, Ros Rinker, author of *Prayer: Conversing with God,* describes prayer as "a dialogue between two persons who love each other." Essential to communion with God is the practice of listening to God.

I do not believe that listening to God was ever meant to be an unattainable, elusive discipline designed strictly for theologians and mature religious leaders. I believe that God intended all men and women of all ages and races to hear His voice and be in relationship with Him. That is the very reason He gave us His word, the Bible. It is accessible and available to everyone. (There are hundreds of organizations whose sole purpose is to translate the Bible in every language and deliver it to remote locations for this very reason.)

I believe that it is through the Bible that you and I can learn of God's unchanging love, power, and plan for all generations. But we must read it.

On an airplane recently, I sat next to the CEO of a nationally known company. We had a wonderful discussion that included everything from books to the differences in the many countries and cultures he had visited. While we were talking about the books we were currently reading, he asked me if I had ever read *The Bible Code*. I had not read that book yet, so I asked him to tell me more about it.

He was very enthusiastic—and curious—about the concept behind the book. I remember paraphrasing his description of the book with, "So, this book seems to point to a Creator?" He gave me a puzzled look.

Then I asked him, "Have you ever read the Bible?"

He said, "No, actually, I never have."

I said, "You really owe it to yourself to read the entire Bible before making any final decisions about God or the validity of the Bible."

Because the Bible includes history, poetry, and parables that detail how God loves all people, interacts with them, and speaks to them, I can't imagine how intellectual people can make a decision or a discovery about God *without* reading the Bible! However, my unofficial poll reveals that most people have never read the *entire* Bible, yet they have preconceived ideas and misconceptions about what it says. They may have heard stories from the Bible in their youth and heard or memorized key verses at one point in their lives, but they have never read the Bible from cover to cover to get the full picture and the complete story of the living, loving God.

I struggled at one time with accomplishing the task of reading such a very thick book. And it wasn't until I was compelled to hear God's voice on a daily basis that I discovered a practical approach to reading the Bible.

At about the same time in 1984 that I decided to pray for one hour each day, a Bible had been published that was divided into 365 daily readings. In order to read through the Bible in a year, you simply had to look up the date and read that date's reading. Each day's reading offered selections from the Old Testament,

New Testament, a few verses from the Book of Proverbs and a Psalm.

So, the natural next step in my conversation with the CEO was to offer to send him a copy of the 365-Day Bible that I have since co-published with Tyndale House Publishers called **The change your life Daily Bible**. He was not offended but delighted with the offer and handed me his business card.

Talk to God, Listen to God

I have personally experienced many extremely exciting and motivating conversations with God using this simple method of talking to God and listening to God. That is why I am compelled and committed to share my experience and system with both believers and seekers alike. I believe that if you will connect with God on a daily basis, it will be the catalyst to change your whole life for the better.

On the **Spiritual** page of **The change your life Daily Journal,** in the **Talk to God** journal space provided, I encourage you to write a letter to God, expressing your thoughts and concerns. Be honest with Him. Share your feelings and your fears. Admit your struggles and ask for His help. Talk to Him about others who need His help as well. Thank Him for something or someone positive in your day. By recording these conversations, you will have written proof that He hears you when you begin to see answers to your prayers. (Remember, there are many ways to answer a request other than with a "yes" response!)

In the **Listen to God** section of this journal page, use the space to record what you believe that God is saying to you on a daily basis. Open your Bible to a familiar chapter or simply locate today's date in **The change your life Daily Bible** and read. I sug-

date _____

talk to God

Today, in honest transparency, share—in writing—your thoughts, gratitude, regrets, fears, plans, hopes, dreams and requests for yourself and others with the living, loving God.

_____
_____
_____
_____
_____
_____
_____
_____
_____
_____
_____
_____
_____
_____
_____
_____
_____
_____

s
p
i
r
i
t
u
a
l

listen to God

God's voice is found in His word, the Bible.
Unless you have another system, read today's **change your life Daily Bible** using Today's Date. Write in this area, any verse or verses that stand out, touch your heart, encourage or correct you. **What is God saying to you today?**

_____
_____
_____
_____
_____
_____

change
your
life
daily

gest that you underline any verse or verses that stand out, touch your heart, or give you direction, correction, and encouragement. Then, rewrite that verse or verses, or paraphrase them in your own words.

Because I have been so positively and powerfully changed through my daily appointments with God, I want everyone to experience how simple yet life-changing it is to connect with the living, loving God, including my college-aged son.

My son has a wonderful, amusing and charming personality. Everything he does is filtered through a "fun" meter. So, you can only imagine how growing up in the home of an advocate of abstinence from alcohol has been for such a child. Because I was an alcoholic, and the child of an alcoholic, I have always been very open with Jake about the possibility that exists for him to become addicted to alcohol.

Unfortunately, drinking alcohol has been, and remains to be, the activity of choice for millions of high school and college students. In fact, it may even be more of a problem for this generation of students than it was twenty or even ten years ago. Kids and adults are made to believe that if you don't drink, you don't have as much fun. We see the advertisements (drink the right beer and you'll get the beautiful girl), and watch it in the movies (romantic evenings on the silver screen always seem to include wine or champagne). The message is repeatedly given: alcohol = fun.

My greatest fear is that Jake will get caught up with alcohol. My deepest desire is for him to fully enjoy his life, without falling into the drinking patterns that I, as well as my father, aunt, and grandfather, fell into.

As parents, we try as long as our kids live in our home, to maintain a certain level of influence and control. But when they go off to college, our children determine their own choices and, ultimately, their destiny. As did my son.

His first semester at college was probably more wild than I will ever know. But I didn't have any reason to suspect that it was until January 1. He was home for winter break and had planned to spend New Year's Eve with all of his friends who were home from college.

In high school, Jake did not have a curfew. We had certain agreements to which he adhered, allowing us to have a great deal of trust and respect for him.

So, when he didn't come home on New Year's Eve, I thought he probably felt that it would be safer to just stay at a friend's home, rather than drive home in the early morning when the roads could be full of drunk New Year's Eve revelers.

By noon on January 1, I had not even heard from Jake, but still considered that his behavior was pretty normal for a college kid who had spent the evening with his friends. By 5:00 P.M., I wasn't happy. In fact, I was angry. I felt that Jake should have at least called us by then, if not made a point of coming home early enough in the day so we could celebrate the new year as a family. I simply didn't understand his behavior. So, I began to call around to his friends' homes. I was a bit embarrassed, and irritated that all of the parents knew where their kids were, but I did not.

When I located Jake at a friend's house, I said, "What are you doing?" He said, "I'm watching football." Silence. I curtly said, "Come home."

It was still a few more hours before Jake came walking in.

He plopped himself on the couch and said nothing.

I looked at his dad, who was sitting on a couch across the room. I gave Roger the "say something" look, but he said nothing. In fact, he was speechless and rather emotional.

I, on the other hand, was not feeling speechless. I wanted to say a hundred things. But all I said was, "Where were you all night?"

He said, "I just want you to know that I don't live here any-more and you can't tell me what to do. I'm in college now, and I have a lot of decisions to make about my life—by myself."

I wanted to shout and cry and demand that Jake go back to being the compliant, obedient child that he had been in high school. But I knew I couldn't do that. Instead, I moved over to the couch where Jake was sitting and I got down on my knees beside him. I said, "Jake, I know that you are in college. And I understand you want to make these decisions about life by your-self. They are very important, not just for now, but they will affect your entire life. So, I am going to pray and fast for you as you make these decisions."

Jake replied, "I want you to."

I realized in that moment that Jake was not rebellious. He was testing and experimenting to see if what he had been taught and seen modeled throughout his childhood was valid, and if it was the way in which he wanted to live his adult life.

Quick to take advantage of this teaching moment and his willing spirit, I added, "Jake, **The change your life Daily Bible** begins on January 1. Would you be willing to read the Bible to hear God's perspective on these life decisions, since you really don't want our advice?"

He said, "Yeah, I would." He wasn't running. He was search-ing. I gave him a brand-new Bible.

The following morning, I arose and grabbed my journal and Bible. I have found that the best way for me to find peace in dif-ficult situations is to immediately write down all of my thoughts, anxieties, and fears and share them with the Lord. I don't always receive immediate solutions, but I always sense that God hears me, is involved in my life, has a plan that will unfold, is always present, and desires to meet with me.

When I turned to the **Talk to God** section of the **Spiritual** journal page, I didn't have enough space to write all of my feelings. But I was honest. I poured out my fears to God.

I wrote, "Lord, how can this be? Jake is falling apart! He's falling right into the trap I fell into with drinking! What can I do?"

Then, I opened **The change your life Daily Bible** to January 2 and I read the chapters of the Old and New Testaments and the Psalm. Then as if a neon light was flashing at me, I read the following verses from that day's reading from the Book of Proverbs: "Listen, my child, to what your father teaches you. Don't neglect your mother's teaching. What you learn from them will crown you with grace and clothe you with honor" (NLT, Proverbs 1:8–9).

I sat quietly, and then wrote out that verse in the **Listen to God** journal section. A peace filled my heart. God was speaking to both me and Jake.

The next day's reading in Proverbs said, "My child, if sinners entice you, turn your back on them! They may say, 'Come and join us. Let's hide and kill someone . . .' Don't go along with them, my child! . . . Stay far away from their paths" (NLT, Proverbs 1:10–15).

I was, once again, impressed by God's way of using His word to speak to my child. It became my greater goal to simply encourage my son to find direction for his life through God's word, the Bible.

The months that followed were quiet. Rog and I were not involved in Jake's daily life. When we did talk with him, many times we came to an impasse. I continued to pray for my son to hear God's voice while he was making such important decisions. And as he was making these decisions, he knew that we were praying for him, encouraging him, and always loving him.

On Mother's Day, I was flying home from a wedding with Roger. I made the comment that it was Mother's Day and I hadn't gotten even a card from Jake. I wondered where he was, what he was doing, if he was avoiding me. My husband could not really console me.

When we deplaned, Jake was standing at the gate with three different, bright flowers that he had chosen himself from a local florist to give to me. He had even called the dog sitter to find out when we would be arriving and drove the one and a half hours from his college to meet our plane at the gate.

With very few words, Jake's gesture spoke volumes to me. He was appreciative of the way we were prayerfully letting him discover his own faith.

One of my greatest desires is to have an open and honest relationship with my son. I want to be able to talk to him and listen to him. That, I believe, is exactly how God, the Father, feels toward me. He wants me to be as open and honest with Him as a loved child can be with their parent. He wants me to talk to Him, not be afraid of Him, but to express my every fear, doubt, pain, and confession. And He wants me to listen to and follow His advice. Over and over, He has proven to me that I can daily hear His voice. In fact, I never have to search farther than a Bible if I want to know God's will or plan for my life.

One of the most poignant memories I have of listening to God occurred on April 27, 1996.

One week earlier, my father had a massive heart attack, and all three of his children had flown from California to Cleveland to be by his side. We were told that his condition was very serious and that his quality of life might be severely impaired if he lived.

We wanted to see him improve, regain his health, and then move to California so that we would all be near each other. Dad really didn't want to move to California. He had lived in Cleveland all of his life and loved his job as the bookkeeper for the same youth organization I had worked for in Cleveland.

The night of April 26, I was alone with my father at the hospital. We watched the Cleveland Indians game together—rooting, laughing, and relishing their victory. This was the first night that week in which I was going to sleep at our family home, rather than at the hospital. I asked Dad if I could pray with him. As we folded our hands together, I asked the Lord to be near my dad, to help him not be afraid.

When I was done praying, I left the room as the night nurse was coming to prepare my dad for sleep. As I walked down the hallway, I heard my father ask the nurse, "Did you hear that nice prayer my daughter just prayed for me?"

Those were the last words I ever heard my father say. On the following morning, April 27, my father died in his sleep.

I called my husband and son in California to give them the sad news. Later that afternoon, Roger called me back and asked me if I had I read today's reading in **The change your life Daily Bible.**

"No," I answered. I hadn't even stopped to sit down, as there had been so many details and decisions to make that day.

He said, "Becky, you don't want to miss hearing God's voice today."

The last verse of the New Testament reading for April 27 from Luke 23:43 reads, "And Jesus replied, 'I assure you, today you will be with me in paradise'" (NLT).

Every year, when I turn to the April 27 reading, I fondly remember how that verse had impacted me on the day my father died. It was a powerful experience to read a verse—and hear God's voice—on the very day that my father passed from his earthly life. It gave me immeasurable comfort, hope, and peace. It was as if Jesus, Himself, was speaking to me, giving me assurance that my dad was with Him in paradise, and that one day I would be with them both!

I knew that my father was in heaven, not because he had earned his way there, but because he had put his faith and trust in the living, loving God—just as I had many years earlier. It is one of my most cherished memories to know that my parents accepted my conversion experience as credible. They did not reject the changed—and very spiritual—person who I was when I came home from California, but they embraced my exuberant faith. They even went with me to my new church. This wasn't easy for them to do. But I had lived in their home, struggled for years with drugs and alcohol, and when I attributed my new ways and new life to God, they had to agree that only something or Someone supernatural could have turned my life around so abruptly. They could see that I did not possess a religion but that I had had a life-changing encounter with the living, loving God. And although they were in their fifties and had been churchgoers all their lives, my parents not only accepted me, but they validated my transformation by opening their hearts to God with the same simple prayer that the janitor had prayed with me.

Do you truly want to change your life?

to balance the "out-of- balance" areas?
to resolve and heal certain relationships?
to fulfill the dreams and goals that are within your heart?
to feel God's love and presence in your every day?
to become a difference-maker in this confused world?

I am *convinced* that you will change your life if you will decide to have *daily written conversations* where you talk to God and listen to Him. For it is in a daily encounter with the living, loving God that you will get your "marching orders."

SEVEN

Make It Happen (Mental)

Detail Your Day
Define Your Dream

BENEFIT: *When you follow a daily, written action plan based on your designated priorities, you are taking practical steps toward defining your dreams and fulfilling your purpose in life.*

TRUTH: *You* can *change your life with 8 Daily To Do's.*

I have journaled for at least one hour a day for over fifteen years and attribute so much of my success and happiness in these years to this one daily discipline. Yet, I can narrow it down to one practical reason that I have been successful in this accomplishment. I have looked at my calendar, one day ahead, and located the first uninterrupted hour of that next day. That hour becomes a scheduled (penciled in) appointment on my calendar—an appointment with myself.

I protect and guard that appointment by not "double booking" other appointments during that time. In addition, I am prepared for it. I always have extra journal supplies on hand, spare pen refills, and appropriate music available to cover any unexpected noise around me. I also set an alarm to ring one hour after I have started. I find that setting an amount of time for my appointment forces me to slow down and resist rushing.

I really believe that the simple habit of choosing what time my appointment will be—one day in advance—has been the reason that I have been able to accumulate over five thousand hours of journaling about all aspects of my life.

The fact that I have always used a journal that is structured, rather than free flowing, has also given me a sense of focus, purpose, and direction in all four areas of my life. Instead of only feeling better, I also walk away with no less than three action steps that I want to carry out, and often times, as many as twenty.

As I begin to journal each day in **The change your life Daily Journal,** I start on the **Physical** page. This is where I record what I plan to eat and when I plan to exercise today *and* tomorrow. At this point, I often turn to the same day's **Mental** page and note the time when I have to leave for the gym and the time I will be back to the home or office. I also transfer this information to my week- or month-at-a-glance calendar, so that I can see if this plan will fit into both my day and week, or if there is a conflict. This gives me an opportunity to immediately schedule an alternate workout at another time later that day at my home with a video or at the gym.

I return to the **Physical** page and consider how I will eat right today. Because I have a different travel and work schedule every week, I really have to plan my meals one day ahead to maintain balance in the physical area of my life. For instance, some Thursdays I have to catch an early flight. This means I will be eating airplane food unless I pick up a healthy turkey sandwich at the deli on Wednesday night, pack it in my carry-on bag, and take it on the plane.

During weeks when I am home, I can often work out at my preferred times and eat healthy food without a lot of extra planning and preparation. But if I have an unexpected interruption or meeting, I must always have an alternate plan.

On the **Emotional** page of **The change your life Daily Journal,** I write in the space provided exactly how I will **Forgive** and **Give** that day. Very often, both of those journal entries create activities for me to transfer onto the **Mental** page of my journal or onto a To Do list for the day. For example, almost daily I will write down that I need to call a friend, write a letter to someone to thank them for a special kindness, or send an E-mail to someone who has come to my mind during my journal time. Again, I quickly turn to the **Mental** page of my journal or to a daily To Do list and jot down those specifics.

Even as I **Talk to God** and **Listen to God** on the **Spiritual** page of my journal, I will often write about a specific passion for a person or project. Whether I am prompted to share something, give someone a verbal encouragement, or send an organization money, I have found that the most efficient and foolproof way to complete these tasks is to transfer the specific action steps onto the **Mental** page of **The change your life Daily Journal.**

There is a special trick to staying focused during a journal appointment. It begins with writing down the the thoughts and ideas that come to mind on the various "balanced life" pages of your journal, then transferring them into succinct action steps by placing them on the **Mental** page, to be done at a specific time. This three-tier process—(1) journal about the idea, (2) transfer the idea into steps on a "to do" list, and (3) complete them at the appointed time—acknowledges a good idea and turns it into an action step that can be achieved in a timely and realistic pace.

The Fourth and Final Page of Your Daily, Written Action Plan

It has been said that you cannot plough a field by turning it over in your mind, and that good intentions will fail the best of us. Therefore, I believe that if you desire increased discipline, organization, or structure in one or more areas of your life, you must design and follow an individualized, daily, written action plan that will focus on bringing balance to all areas of your life, rather than to only one area.

I have designed the **Mental** page of **The change your life Daily Journal** to be the fourth and final page of your daily journal experience. It is the place where you can organize and **Detail Your Day** based on the priorities that you have journaled about on your three previous journal pages.

On the **Mental** page of the **Daily Journal** (or if you make your own journal, this would be a daily To Do List), you should always record when you plan to exercise, spend time with God, and how you plan to implement any other action steps that come to mind during the **Eat Right, Exercise Regularly, Forgive, Give, Talk to God,** and **Listen to God** journal sections.

As you design your daily, written action plan, it is imperative to include a month or week-at-a-glance calendar in your planning efforts. **The change your life Daily Journal** provides sixty days of daily journal pages and two month-at-a-glance calendars. When you are planning activities for today, a quick look at a monthly calendar allows you to see a more realistic and complete picture of your week and month. It will help you better manage and prioritize each day, week, and month. In addition, continu-

date _____

m
e
n
t
a
l

detail your day

appointments

quiet time	☐
work out	☐
	☐
	☐
	☐
	☐
	☐
	☐
	☐
	☐
	☐
	☐
	☐
	☐
	☐
	☐
	☐

calls to make   *phone #*

_____
_____
_____
_____
_____

letters to write/fax/email
                              w f e
_____ ☐ ☐ ☐
_____ ☐ ☐ ☐
_____ ☐ ☐ ☐
_____ ☐ ☐ ☐

things to do

_____ ☐
_____ ☐
_____ ☐
_____ ☐
_____ ☐

define your dream

What is one practical step you can take toward reaching a goal—
and fulfilling a dream—in one or more areas of your life?
Use this space to brainstorm or to develop a dream that won't go away!

physical	emotional
mental	spiritual

change
your
life
daily

ous review of a calendar allows you to immediately notice when your life is in danger of being out of balance.

Think of the **Detail Your Day** section of the **Mental** journal page as a daily worksheet. Its purpose is to help you lead an effective, productive life by reminding you of the tasks and appointments that you consider important. As you set and keep appointments, make phone calls, write letters, and meet deadlines, you will begin to *feel* balance and achievement in your life. You will notice that your relationships become more healthy, your physical fitness improves, and the spiritual aspect of your life improves as a result of following the 8 Daily To Do's.

The change your life Daily Journal is designed to keep you from becoming a workaholic, martyr, or out-of-control person. As you **Detail Your Day,** you will be able to discern what activities might have to be dropped, what patterns have to change, and, more important, when to say "no." By implementing those changes, you are protecting your desire to achieve a balanced life.

Following a written, daily action plan will not always mean that you will complete 100% of your goals or projects. But your life will become *more balanced* as you learn to adjust your schedule to reflect your priorities.

Your Day Is Not Yours Alone

As you **Detail Your Day,** especially if you are a parent, you must expect that your family priorities and responsibilities will regularly interrupt your best-laid plans.

For instance, if your child is in school, you can usually plan to have more personal or professional time during the day, *unless* one of the children gets sick and needs to stay home. On those days, you need to have a backup plan and/or an understanding work environment. If your child needs help with homework, you should try to plan for less personal or professional time in the evening. When your child or children are out of school for breaks or vacations, you will find that your schedule includes not only your own but other children's schedules and plans as well!

If your day is filled with kids, carpools, and cooking enough to feed an army in shifts, then time for journaling, workouts, and your appointment with God will have to be scheduled in the early or later hours of the day—or they will never happen.

If you travel for business, you will have to develop a completely different workout and personal schedule for when you are on the road. It will also mean that you must plan in advance what to pack, and even when to drop off and pick up clothes from the dry cleaner. (I have found that having duplicates of toiletries and other items saves time and frustration.)

If you are going to experience a major change in your life, such as marriage, relocating, or starting a new job, the best thing you can do is sit down and evaluate—in writing—what changes you will need to make in *every* area of your life. Specific issues need to be considered, such as joining a new gym, opening a checking account at a bank in a more convenient location, and even anticipating increased drive time. This will allow you to keep your daily schedule running smoothly during the time of transition. The simple procedure of planning in writing will help you to eliminate unnecessary stress and avoid the loss of time or money that is a result of poor planning.

Do not fall into the trap of saying "yes" to every good opportunity that comes your way. I have been motivated to think differently about the path to achievement by E. Stanley Jones who said, "Your capacity to say no determines your capacity to say yes to greater things." The more diligent you are to design and follow a daily, written action plan that is based on your desired priorities (changes, values, needs, family responsibilities, etc.), the more likely you will be able to achieve your desired goals and overcome your weaknesses.

If you will be realistic and anticipate that your daily action plan might have to change on any day of the week, or at any minute of the day, you will be able to make unavoidable adjustments more quickly and efficiently—and with a better attitude. Rather than repeatedly getting frustrated by interruptions, expect them to come into your life and be prepared to face them with patience, grace, and an alternate plan.

Define Your Dream

The last of the 8 Daily To Do's is called **Define Your Dream.** On the bottom half of the **Mental** journal page, you are encouraged to actively brainstorm and further develop the dreams that are in your heart and won't go away. If you have your own journal, this could be a blank page where you journal about great ideas, personal or professional goals, and childhood aspirations. If you take a few minutes every day to write your personal mission statement or journal about a specific area in your life that you would like to improve, you increase your desire as well as gain momentum to see your dreams become reality.

In this section of your journal, your only task is to dream and brainstorm. This space never has to be seen by anyone; therefore, don't discount any ideas! No one can reject you. Lack of money or negative criticism can't touch your dream. Journaling daily about a dream will increase your interest in it, give you additional insight and perspective, and give you fresh momentum to achieve it.

Simply observe, as the days go by, if your dream or idea grows stronger or weaker. I once heard a pastor say, "If God puts a dream in your heart, it won't go away!" So, don't try to talk yourself into or out of an idea. And don't be afraid to dream big. *You* may not have the financial or physical means to complete a dream, but God is not limited by lack of money or manpower.

And remember, not all dreams are for now! Hindsight proves that most accomplishments take more time than we anticipated. Never giving up or letting go of them is essential to their completion. Whether you are physically constructing something, emotionally working toward healing a relationship, or battling the bulges of your body, when forward progress stalls, the character-building qualities of patience, perseverance, and passion are critical to helping you hold on to your dream.

A dream might begin with an idea or a desire to fill a need. If you keep searching, trying, knocking on doors, believing in and revising your dream, you *will* find a way to be successful. Dreams do and can become a reality for those who persevere. It may not happen in the time frame you prefer, or in the way that you imagined, but your dream is more likely to become a reality if you don't give up.

Reach for the Stars

The **Define Your Dream** section of the **Mental** journal page also provides a place for recording a tangible, practical step toward accomplishing a larger task. You are prompted to daily choose one area of your life—physical, emotional, spiritual, mental—and decide to take a step toward changing or improving that area. There are boxes to check if you would like to complete this step today, this week, this month, or this year. This section has the power to push you toward your dream.

In the summer of 1997, I wrote down a dream in my journal. I wanted to develop a Web site. I am not a technical person, nor am I very patient with complicated concepts such as the Internet. But I was certain that the Internet is an incredibly expeditious way to communicate your message to millions of people anywhere in the world. Although I was not sure how to do this, I just couldn't let go of the idea.

I began to journal in the summer about having a Web site, but it took me until September of 1997 to call a friend who designed Web sites. Each time we spoke, he would give me what seemed to be one more overwhelming task. It took many weeks to accomplish just one step. First, I had to register a domain name. I didn't know who to call, much less what to name my domain. Then I had to find a server to host my Web site. Each call took an incredible amount of time because I had to have every person explain everything in lay terms. In addition, I spent hours making creative decisions regarding the design of my site. And when I thought I had it all completed, I needed to call the telephone company to acquire more phone lines!

Every day I would journal about the next step in the **Define Your Dream** section of my journal. I was always asking and answering the question, "What is the next step that I need to take to have a Web site for my company that will allow me to communicate my message and mission to millions?"

We were up and running in 1997, and over the past three years I have improved my Web site two more times, giving it new and improved technical capabilities. *www.changeyourlifedaily.com* has gone from a few simple pages to a secured order site with a fresh, daily "tip" to encourage you, a monthly update to motivate you, a guest book, and a weekly "on-line" **change your life Group**!

It all began with a dream that I wrote down in my journal.

Step after step (and had I known how many steps, I might not have gotten started), I tackled and pursued this dream until it became a reality.

The Power of Your Written Word

I am sure that you have discovered that a good intention is not enough to empower you to fulfill your goals and dreams.

When something has remained on your "to do" list for too long, I encourage you to recognize this as a good idea or intention that you have not become serious about achieving. To push you toward action, ask yourself . . .

- How long do I think this will take to accomplish?
- When is the first time my calendar has that much free time?
- Is there any information that I need, or any articles/resources I need to purchase, borrow, or retrieve before I can begin?
- Is this too difficult to do alone? Who could I ask to come along with me for moral support?
- Am I embarrassed or ashamed for certain people to know that I am attempting this change, admitting this weakness, or needing help?
- If this project will take more time than I think I have now, how can I divide this project into two, five, or ten steps that can be accomplished one step or day or hour at a time?
- Where can I keep a record of my progress regarding this project, goal, or dream? (examples: in a file, in a drawer at home or work, on my computer, in my journal, etc.)

- Who can keep me accountable to make this change, reach this goal, or complete this "to do"? (examples: a secretary, boss, child, friend, spouse, **change your life Group** member, sponsor, or personal trainer)
- Will this help other people?
- Will I be fulfilled if I do not attempt this?

As you ask and answer these questions, perhaps you will become more honest with yourself about your dream and become more willing to do what it takes to achieve it.

I am absolutely convinced that the most effective way to achieve change and balance in your life is through a daily, written action plan. I can attribute the significant changes in my life to over fifteen years of *daily*—not sporadic or haphazard, but *daily*—journaling. That is why I encourage you to journal every single day. It is a powerful self-motivation and discovery tool.

If you avoid writing down your thoughts, ideas, and prayers, you should ask yourself "Why?" Is it a time issue? Do you think that your idea will take too much effort, last too long, be too difficult, create too big of a mess, hurt someone's feelings, or cost you something that you don't want to pay? Do you procrastinate ever, sometimes, or rarely? Are you afraid of success or failure?

Journaling is a practical, nonthreatening method for overcoming your fears and achieving desired change in your life.

You have come this far, yet there is one more step. It is my deepest conviction that awareness, admission, and a daily action plan are still not enough to sustain you for life on the journey of change. I believe that you and I simply cannot maintain long-lasting change without accountability.

EIGHT

Change Is Sustained with Accountability

For many years, I have taken the same route to walk my dog. Regularly, on one particular street I would see and wave to the same cute mom who was in her early thirties. There were always kids, animals, and toys in the front yard—signs of a happy American family.

There was another sign that I detected. There seemed to be a sad longing in her eyes. Was she was searching for something? I couldn't tell for what or why, but I had an inkling that I might be able to relate to her. I wondered if she was feeling helpless or if her life was spinning out of control. I seemed to sense she had a great deal of hidden or unspoken pain. Finally, I decided that there was only one way to find out if I was on the right track. There was a big chance that she would reject me, that I would humiliate myself, but for twenty-four years I have been compelled to reach out to strangers with the same simple message that changed my life.

One morning, on my daily dog walk, I went up to her doorbell, rang it, and found her at home. We both seemed a little embarrassed, but I introduced myself as a neighbor—and speaker—and wondered if she would like to be my guest at an event where I would be telling my story of how faith had changed my life.

The moment the words came out of my mouth, I thought, "How tacky can you get, Becky, inviting someone to hear YOU speak?"

I was dumbfounded when, without hesitation, she excitedly responded to my invitation with, "Yes, I would love to go. I will arrange a babysitter and go with you."

We chatted some more and I walked away and tucked away the thought that it soon might be my turn to be a janitor in someone else's life. As I turned the corner, I realized I didn't even know her last name or phone number, so I couldn't even call her to give her the details of the event. The next day I walked over to her house with a note, which included my phone number, and left it in her mailbox. Kendra called that night to confirm.

The following Saturday morning I drove over and picked up my new friend and we chatted easily as we drove the short distance to the event. Since I would be staying after to greet people and sign books, I arranged a ride home for her with another friend. On Monday, while on my daily dog walk, I was anxious to visit with her and find out what she thought of my speech. As I approached her house, I was delighted to see Kendra standing in the yard. She thanked me for inviting her to the event and said she enjoyed my presentation. She was very sweet, and I was glad that I made a new friend.

The following week, we talked regularly. I could tell that we were both making an effort to see each other on a daily basis. I could also tell that she was trying to share something with me.

One warm summer morning, a few weeks later, we stood chatting on her front lawn. Amidst kids, toys, and animals, my neighbor poured her heart out to me. Before she vulnerably admitted the addiction with which she was struggling, she said, "No one knows this about me, but after hearing you speak, I knew that you would understand."

My first reaction to her confession was to offer her the only solution I knew could bring her immediate relief from her guilt, as well as provide hope for her future. Since she knew my story, I asked her if she would allow me to be the "janitor" in her life and introduce her to God in a simple prayer. I continued to explain that all she had to do was to ask Him to come into her life, forgive her, and help her.

She shared that she knew that she would need daily, if not hourly, support and accountability to get through the first ninety days of sobriety and abstinence. I knew that I was not able to be there for her daily, as I traveled quite frequently. So, I offered to come by her house every day that I was home during the summer and pray for her, just as I had done that morning. She admitted that praying out loud was a new experience for her, but she was comfortable with me and could tell that I genuinely believed that prayer would help her.

As we discussed the need for additional daily support, I assured her that, although God was unseen, He would be there for her through His word, found in the Bible. I encouraged her to journal and read the Bible daily. I promised to bring over both resources to her later that day.

We also agreed that she would need the added support of an accountability group. She explained that she was familiar with Twelve Step meetings in the community and confessed that she had tried many times before to tackle her addiction. She admitted that she had previously tried to find sobriety without a complete and total surrender to God.

We had a very thorough plan. For the next ninety days, in addition to attending one or two recovery meetings per day, she would journal her conversations with God, read the Bible, and pray often with a *spiritual* sponsor—me!

After hundreds of daily meetings and many written prayers, Kendra has achieved many months of sobriety and I am very proud of her.

A Group Is to Support and Encourage You

In all my years of sobriety, I had never attended a traditional meeting for alcoholics—*as* an alcoholic. I had gone to a meeting *before* I considered myself an alcoholic, and ten years ago I had attended a meeting with a woman friend who had asked me to go with her. But on the week of my twentieth anniversary of marriage and sobriety in January of 1998, I called Kendra, my neighbor. I inquired about where I might find a local meeting for alcoholics. I told her that I wasn't really sure why I wanted to attend a meeting this particular week, but I was compelled, curious, and somewhat driven to have this experience.

Kendra was rather surprised but seemed pleased that I would be willing and open to attend a traditional meeting for alcoholics. I was familiar with the Twelve Steps, as the church I attended held similar recovery groups for teens and adults, of which I had even been a facilitator. But I sensed that attending a traditional meeting for alcoholics—as a participant—held a different meaning.

Kendra suggested that as a "first-timer," I should attend an evening woman's meeting, which was held weekly in a cute home near the ocean. She told me that she found "home" meetings more cozy and friendly. Because she was a busy mom and evening meetings were not very convenient for her, she would not be able to accompany me, but she offered to call ahead and ask the hostess to keep an eye out for a first-timer who would be coming alone.

It was too late now. I was committed. I wondered, "Do I *really* want to do this? *Why* do I want to do this—and alone?"

I decided that I really *didn't* want to go alone to a meeting for the first time, so I asked another good friend if she would go with me. Neither of us knew what to expect or how to act. When we walked in the room and didn't know anyone, we chatted quietly with each other, smiled at the women already seated, and waited.

Before the meeting officially opened, the woman who lived in the house where we were meeting leaned over my shoulder and melodically sang out the name, "Spirit." I held my breath, looked to the left and right, and felt my body tense up. At that moment, I wasn't sure if we were going to be chanting mantras or singing songs to spirits! I was honestly a bit worried that I might have made a mistake in coming to this traditional meeting for alcoholics. Just then, a white, fluffy animal whisked by my knees and shins responding to her master's affectionate call.

"Whew," I whispered. I felt embarrassed but mostly relieved that I had overreacted.

The meeting began on time and we were asked to introduce ourselves. A ritual at a traditional meeting for alcoholics is to say your name, followed by the phrase, "I'm an alcoholic . . ."

Before I left for the meeting that night, my husband advised me that this type of introduction was procedure, and he was quite curious to know if I was going to introduce myself in that way. I told him that I didn't *know* how I was going to introduce myself. I didn't usually make it a habit to introduce myself as an alcoholic to strangers. I usually say, "I'm an author and speaker!" (He just smiled, as if he knew something I didn't . . .)

When the moment came for me to introduce myself, I said,

"My name is Becky and I'm an alcoholic." I realized that there was much more to my life than this one statement, but it was a very vulnerable and self-descriptive label that each woman in the room (besides my friend whom I dragged along) held in common. Through this humbling admission, we each shared our struggle to be honest about our alcoholism.

Looking around, you might guess that some of us in the room were in the beginning stages of our recovery, while others of us had been sober for many years. It was a poignant and powerful moment to sit knee-to-knee with perfect strangers and share one's vulnerability, weaknesses, and imperfections.

Next, as a part of the tradition of the organization, the group read the Twelve Steps out loud.

Then the assigned leader for the evening asked the "chip" chairman to stand up. Because there had been a plentiful array of snack foods on the table, I looked over at the table and thought, "Taco chips? Potato chips?" I wasn't exactly sure to what or whom they were referring. Did they mean the refreshment chairman?

It became clear to me when a woman stood up and held up a round engraved token that she called a "chip." A chip was a coin given as an award, a symbol or a mark of one's achievement.

First, a "desire" chip was offered to anyone who desired to be sober for thirty days. How encouraging, I thought, for those who have not yet found success in their daily struggle to be given something tangible to hold on to as hope until they reached thirty days of sobriety.

Chips were given out and received with pride in increments of thirty, sixty, and ninety days and then one, two, and five years of sobriety. Each woman who earned a chip was also given a hug. The longer achievements were celebrated with flowers and a card.

Not wanting to overlook anyone or a special anniversary, the "chip" chairman asked, "Is anyone else celebrating an anniversary we haven't named?"

I briefly thought about her question. As a first-timer, I had only been observing and enjoying the experience, not expecting to be part of it. Then it occurred to me, "Could this be the reason I felt so strongly about coming to a meeting this week?" I had reached a true mile marker in sobriety circles!

I slowly and almost shyly raised my hand.

The "chip" chairman politely asked, "And what anniversary are you celebrating?" The entire roomful of women turned to look at me, the "first-timer."

I was almost embarrassed to say the number at first. I wondered if my achievement would seem less important because I had not been a part of their group, sharing my steps and struggles with them.

It was too late to be quiet now, so I spoke up, "Tonight is my twentieth anniversary of sobriety. And although I have never been a part of traditional meetings for alcoholics, I am coming tonight to find continued healing and spiritual growth in my life."

The group immediately let out a roar, a round of applause, and then someone shouted out, "Wow, twenty years! I have a cake in the car. We'll bring it in and celebrate after the meeting!"

I was stunned and thrilled. I was also inspired by the warm response from these women whom I had just met. Some were much younger than I was, and a few were older. There was an equal mixture of single and married women. But each of them supported me with their applause and smiles. I did not feel like a "first-timer." I felt welcomed and encouraged!

I immediately sensed that my achievement, twenty years of sobriety, was a shared victory for all of us in the room.

One woman asked, "How did you do it without the Twelve Steps?"

Those who receive chips commemorating special anniversaries are given a few minutes to speak. With an odd nervousness for a woman who made her living as a speaker, I shared that I *had* been regularly and actively involved in a variety of spiritual growth programs in the past twenty years. In fact, I shared that many of the groups had used the Twelve Steps as a design for growth, and all of them had served as my support groups.

But I would have been remiss not to share the most compelling part of my story with my new friends (and captive audience). I told a one-minute version of how a janitor, a complete stranger, had introduced me to God in a simple prayer and how, through that prayer, God had met me—right there. I shared how He had changed my life forever and that I have never been the same since that day.

Every face in the room stared intently at me, waiting for more of the story. With great emotion, I continued, "In that passionate prayer, I begged God to help me and to give me a fresh start. On August 26, 1976, God took away my insatiable desire for alcohol and drugs. But it wasn't until I was alone with a bottle of champagne did I understand that I must make a decision never to drink.

"In fact, today is my twentieth anniversary of sobriety and marriage. It was on my honeymoon that I discovered and admitted to my husband that I will always be an alcoholic. It was also the last time I ever had a drink.

"I have to thank God for getting me through the toughest days of withdrawal, and for giving me a husband who, on our honeymoon, made a decision to abstain from alcohol with me—and we have done so every day for the past twenty years.

"If I had time to tell you my whole story, you would see that my life has taken the path that the Twelve Steps are based upon. When I admitted that I couldn't control my life without God's help, I turned my whole life over to Him and the healing began. I learned to admit my shortcomings to God and others and to ask for forgiveness daily. Spending time with God daily has kept me passionate about telling others of His love and healing power."

The "chip" chairman began rummaging wildly through her chip box. She seemed flustered and said, "Well, let's see . . . I don't even think that I stock twenty-year chips! I'll have to pick one up at the supply store this week! But I do have a one-year chip and a ten-year chip, neither of which you've received before today!"

I took the chips in my hand and held them like I had once held my prized synchronized swimming medals. I was so proud of this achievement.

The meeting continued with the group reading aloud from a book about alcoholics that was written many years ago. The reading consisted of guidelines for emotional, relational, and physical healing and growth. Who *couldn't* use this type of advice?

At the end of the meeting, I looked more closely at one side of my ten-year chip. It said, "Keep coming back!" On my way to the first meeting, I never really thought about returning to subsequent weekly meetings. At evening's end, the youngest girl in the room came up to me and said, "Please come back." I knew then that my journey of sobriety would include a few more meetings!

When my girlfriend and I got in the car, we shared our thoughts and impressions. I was grateful that she had joined me, but I was certain that I could return to the group the following week on my own. I had made new friends who shared similar struggles and were sojourners with me in a lifelong process of change.

When my husband and I got into bed that night, he said,

"Well, how did it go? By the way, how did you introduce yourself?"

I knew he was waiting for every juicy detail, so I didn't prolong his curiosity. I said, "My name is Becky and I'm an alcoholic."

He replied sincerely, "I'm proud of you." (Perhaps he knew that for every moment that I appear proud and strong, at my core, I still have room to grow and heal.)

I had to brag, "By the way, next week I'm going to get a twenty-year chip for my achievement!" I retold the exciting "chip" part of the meeting and I boasted of how I had received a one-year chip and a ten-year chip, since twenty-year chips were not given out very often!

The humorous and loving guy that he is, replied, "Well, while you're at it, next week pick me up a twenty-year chip. I earned one, too!" We couldn't stop laughing for quite a few minutes.

I am very fortunate to have married a man who would sacrifice for me, support me, and who was not embarrassed or ashamed to be married to a woman who will always be an alcoholic.

But not everyone who struggles with an addiction finds such wonderful encouragement so close to home. I attribute much of my healing and resolve to change to Roger.

But at that Twelve Step meeting on my twentieth anniversary of marriage and sobriety, I learned a very valuable lesson. Not everyone has a Roger. Not everyone's family understands addiction. Not everyone can make it through withdrawal without hourly support. Not everyone is strong enough to battle temptation without a sponsor or a support group. Not everyone is broken enough, or courageous enough, or fed up enough to attend a traditional Twelve Step group. Not everyone is willing to risk their reputation or job to fight for and find healing. Not everyone is able to give up what they have grown to love for what is right or best or prudent or honorable—without help.

I know well enough that most of us struggle with issues that paralyze certain areas of our lives. Yet, even though we may be aware that we need to change, and have admitted to ourselves, God, and others that we want to change, we would never attend a traditional Twelve Step group or a recovery group where we would be recognized or labeled. Neither would we blurt out our weaknesses to our friends at work or church or in our neighborhood. And even if we had a daily action plan, most of us wouldn't tell anyone what it was, in case we failed.

Accountability groups have helped millions to overcome addiction to drugs, alcohol, overeating, sex, and gambling. But for every person who attends one of those groups, many more of us do not.

But without accountability, the majority of us will:

- fail repeatedly,
- attempt to minimize our problem and the pain it is causing,
- rationalize, or
- deny the reality of a situation rather than succeed in making desired, positive changes in our lives.

Believing that everyone needs a safe and confidential place to be encouraged and share their struggles, I decided to gather my friends, neighbors, and acquaintances and begin a **change your life Group**.

A **change your life Group** is an accountability group that anyone can start—and hundreds have already done so! It is a place to meet—in your home or at work—with others who are willing to be transparent and honest about changes they need and want to make in their lives. It is a place with few rules, except to respect each other with confidentiality. It is not an advice-giving meeting, but a place for reporting your individual progress. It is a friendly group where you will be applauded for your successes and encouraged to press on if you are struggling.

Because we all have individual areas of weakness and strength, each person is simply asked to journal every day, following the pattern of the 8 Daily To Do's in **The change your life Daily Journal.** At the meeting each week, the facilitator (whomever would like to lead and is able to keep the meeting running on time) asks each participant to share their progress in achieving their physical, emotional, spiritual, and mental goals. It is exciting and invigorating. It is challenging and often enlightening.

Because each person in the group is a sojourner on the path toward change, it is not important to hold the specific area that one is hoping to change in common. The common ground is that each person desires to make changes in one or more areas of her life.

For example, if one person struggles with outbursts of anger, she is every bit as vulnerable or embarrassed about her debilitating weakness as is the woman who is struggling with an overeating problem.

In each of my **change your life Groups,** I have found that the group develops a personality of its own. Though we differ in age, race, background, marital status, and employment, we find that our common desire to make lifestyle changes inspires us to be transparent, vulnerable, and open with each other.

When we, as individuals, are tempted to give up, become bored, or get impatient with ourselves or our situation, inevitably someone in our group shares something from their life that offers new insight and observation in the process of change. Without giving advice, their transparency and vulnerability renew our desire to make certain specific changes.

For example, when I shared my list of daily, weekly, and yearly goals with my **change your life Group** it sparked a few similar responses in all of us. My desire to be less selfish was echoed by each member. It reminded us that often, unless someone else admits a weakness, our thoughts and ego don't necessarily "think" up a weakness on its own. Although it may be uncomfortable, we have found it more powerful to share honestly with fellow "change-your-lifers" than to hide or ignore areas of our lives that truly need renewal, rescue, or revitalizing.

The relationships within a **change your life Group** build each woman's confidence, compassion, and camaraderie over time. Jealousy fades, commonalities surface, and transparency is appreciated in each other. Similar to a Twelve Step meeting, shared struggles stir up a team effort to battle our problems together. And when you know that you have to give an honest report of your weekly progress, it prompts you to try harder, make time, prioritize better, and plan ahead. Accountability to the group reminds you that your goal to change *is* manageable, possible, and imminent!

In addition, the honest and often humorous interaction that occurs each week provides each member with a faithful support system to remind them to persevere when things are difficult and to applaud them when they have overcome specific weaknesses or achieved certain goals.

Starting a change your life Group

To form a group, make a list of people whom you think would benefit from committing to a daily journal experience and would be willing to attend a weekly group meeting.

Be creative and think about your neighborhood acquaintances, people whom you've met at the gym or at a local club, coworkers, or even family members. When group members differ in age, race, background, employment, and marital status, amazing dynamics occur.

For example, the second group that I led was comprised of a young, aspiring singer who worked at a local sportswear company, an at-home mother of two teenagers, an employed mother of one infant, and a gorgeous, single woman who I met at the gym. We were each struggling in different areas. As we recognized each other's unique weaknesses, we drew upon our individual strengths to motivate each other to persevere. In the process, we became less self-centered and more tolerant and understanding of each other's struggles.

The camaraderie of the **change your life Group** develops as each person becomes more honest and transparent. And although you desire to succeed in overcoming your own weaknesses and reaching individual goals, you also develop the fine art of caring for others.

Whether you are desperate to improve your life or simply disillusioned or disappointed with your position or place in life (examples: single, financially unstable, emotionally wounded, etc.), embarking on the journey to change is both motivating and rewarding *when it is attempted in the presence of others who care about you.*

Finally, the common goal of achieving positive changes—whether physically, emotionally, spiritually, and/or mentally—will draw you to the weekly meeting, as well as uphold you *during* the week.

The change your life Group Leader

As a **change your life Group Leader,** you do not have to be *perfect*—physically, emotionally, spiritually, or mentally. Your only requirement is to be a person who honestly and vulnerably desires to share his or her struggles and victories with others.

Whether you are just beginning on the path toward change or have been diligently working to achieve balance in your life for many years, your willingness to lead the group will provide a wonderful atmosphere for others to be honest and vulnerable along with you.

Setting the right atmosphere for the **change your life Group** can be achieved by (1) choosing a comfortable *place* for the group to meet, (2) minimal *preparation* before each meeting, (3) stressing *punctuality,* and (4) sharing your *passion* for change with the other members of the group.

PLACE

As the leader, it is important that you provide a comfortable, quiet place for your group to meet each week. I held my first **change your life Group** at my home—around the dining room table. Just before everyone arrived, I turned the telephone answering machine "on" and set the ringer on low. I fed my son and husband and reminded them that I was having friends over—and that we could not be interrupted. I also made sure that my dog had a *big* bone to keep her busy for the entire meeting.

Whether you meet in a home or at an office, the meeting place should be free from "people" traffic, noise, and other interruptions. This provides a comfortable atmosphere for confidential sharing.

My second and third groups grew so large that we moved our meeting from the dining room table into my family room. This group was a bit more relaxed, as people liked to sit on the floor or by the fireplace.

PREPARATION

Preparing for the meeting each week will be more thought provoking than time consuming. An eight-week series of assignments are provided for you in the **change your life Leader's Guide** at the end of this book. These assignments are designed to allow each member to share about the areas of their lives that they would like to change.

As each group develops a personality of its own, you will be surprised and encouraged by the depth of conversation, emotion, and honesty that occurs during your time together. Feel free to add to or substitute questions that fit your leadership style or group dynamics.

The following guidelines will help you prepare for a confidential but fun group meeting. These guidelines worked for my group, but feel free to incorporate new ideas, and, please, let me know how they work!

Group Guidelines
1. The group should consist of at least three, but no more than eight, members, ideally of different stages and ages in life.
2. All members will need a copy of **The change your life Daily Journal** and **The change your life Daily Bible** (or their own journal and Bible).

3. Each person must be willing to make a minimal commitment to journal daily for eight weeks *and* attend a weekly, one-hour meeting.

4. Each week, the group should be reminded to come on time! The meeting should start on time and end on time. The leader should set an alarm to ring five to seven minutes before the end of the hour that will be heard by all.

5. Everything that is discussed during the hour is strictly confidential. The sharing that takes places during the group is never to be shared with others outside of the group.

6. Food is discouraged, as treats and desserts can quickly become the focus of the meeting. Eliminating food also avoids a potential area of struggle for many people. And it definitely minimizes the responsibility of the host.

7. This low-budget and low-maintenance get-together should be so nonthreatening that other group members are motivated to begin a **change your life Group** in their home or at work.

PUNCTUALITY

A very important aspect of the **change your life Group** is *punctuality.* It is important that you, the leader, are committed to starting and ending the meeting on time.

Starting the meeting on time, no matter how many people have arrived, shows respect to those who are prompt and assures each person that they will have the opportunity to share during the hour meeting. (Those who might normally show up five to ten minutes late will quickly realize that they are missing out on hearing about the life of another person.)

In order to stay on track I suggest that:

1. The leader should have an opening comment, a short review of last week's assignment, or a fun question planned for the first five minutes of each meeting.
2. Divide the remaining minutes by the number in attendance, which sets a boundary and/or limit for all to know in advance.
3. Set an alarm to ring five to seven minutes before the end of the hour, which gives notification to the entire group that the meeting is almost over.

It is up to you, the leader, to be sensitive to each person's "sharing" needs during the hour. For instance, one week, someone might be having a particularly difficult time. They might share a bit longer than their allotted time, while someone else will have had an easy week and naturally or graciously fall below their allotted time. On the following week, a different person may be struggling. Your ability to gently move the group along is one of your key responsibilities.

I found that the group counted on me, the leader, to hold the meeting to the designated one hour time frame. Some of the women had other meetings to attend or a babysitter to get back to. In order to keep their commitment to our group, it was important that we respected their other commitments.

PASSION

During the sharing time, the leader is not meant to be an advice giver or a counselor, but simply a *passionate* sojourner on the path to changing his or her life. The most effective facilitators are humble encouragers who don't add sentiment or advice to the end of each person's sharing. I found that simply saying, "Thank you for sharing" or "Thank you for being so transparent" was the type of statement that affirmed each person yet kept the meeting running on time. If someone does not want to share an answer to a specific question, I ask, "Is there anything else you would like to share about during this time?"

The **change your life Group** should be a secure, safe place where members can come to share the areas of their lives that need improvement—without condemnation or fear of exposure. The **change your life Group Leader** is not a teacher or speaker, but a facilitator whose main responsibility is to be sure that each person has a place to share their struggles and goals—and can be encouraged and supported in the process.

Each group member, as well as the leader, should refrain from advice giving, inappropriate language, or gossip.

I strongly discourage advice giving, lengthy commentary, or unrelated discussion during our hour. But when the group is over, gals often stand on the sidewalk and privately give each other a special word of encouragement. Complete confidentiality should be mentioned as a "rule" on a weekly basis. This facilitates genuine vulnerability among the women who are there each week. Each week, you will find that someone different is the focus of the group's encouragement and support.

If you've never been in a small group, I believe that you are truly keeping yourself from great personal growth. A **change your life Group** is designed to be a friendly place where women can come together and feel free to share confidentially what is in their hearts and on their minds.

A Perfect Illustration . . .

One of my friends, Cindy, is a perfect illustration of how a group experience can cause you to define the dream that has been in your heart for a long time.

She shares her story with us . . .

"I have always loved reading and writing. Even when I was in high school I wrote and journaled. After I was married and had two small children, I found that it was therapeutic to write down my thoughts and feelings.

"I loved being a mom, but as the years flew by, I realized that before I knew what hit me, I was going to be an 'empty nester.' I had been active in the church and the community, but for most of my adult years, my daughters were my full-time job. I had a volunteer position for almost fifteen years, speaking to women at 'mothers of preschoolers' groups, and I occasionally did some freelance writing. But, as my children entered their later teen years, I wondered what course my life would take when they left home.

"I had observed several of my friends struggling when their youngest child left for college. They weren't sure what to do, and wished they'd been better prepared. I began to ask God to guide me toward what the next step would be for me.

"I remember saying, 'God, please tell me *now* what you want me to do when Amy leaves for college. Then I can start preparing and planning for it.' He didn't quite shout out an answer as I'd hoped.

"But about that time I became a part of Becky's **change your life Group.** I was already friends with Becky and thoroughly enjoyed our friendship. We had fun together, and our children were friends. In addition, we challenged each other physically on outdoor mountain-bike rides and spiritually, as well.

"Through my daily journal appointments with God, listening to God through the Bible, and through the group, God began to point me toward the next step that He had for me.

"At one of the first meetings we were encouraged to write down short-term and long-term goals in the each of the four balanced life areas. Doing this really forced me to look ahead at the next stage of my life, which was so rapidly approaching. Becky had periodically asked me what my dreams were for the future, and I never knew how to answer. She challenged me to think about it, and the group challenged me to write about it.

"I was a little uncomfortable sharing my dreams, because I was afraid I might fail. But as we talked, prayed, and I read daily in **The change your life Daily Bible,** I realized that I would really like to get into writing more seriously.

"I determined that one of my goals was to start writing articles. Once I voiced that thought out loud, the creative juices went into overdrive. I had so many thoughts and ideas.

"Next, I had the thought to write a weekly column for the newspaper. I would have been embarrassed to share that with most people, but my **change your life Group** was such an 'all for one, and one for all' group that I knew it was safe to share my dream with them.

"I kept writing out my thoughts and ideas in **The change your life Daily Journal.** And because I knew that I would be asked each week how I was doing with the writing, that level of accountability forced me to step out of my comfort zone and take another step toward writing for a newspaper.

"One week I said that I was going to approach the editor of the newspaper. I put it off, but finally made the call because I knew the group would ask me. I also knew that they were praying for me, and rooting for me. I was nervous to make the call, and even more nervous when I went to meet with the editor that October to show him my column ideas.

"I was pleasantly surprised when he said he liked the idea and would get back to me before Thanksgiving. I didn't hear a thing from him, but I did sense that God was gently reminding me that He had a perfect timing for this. I didn't hear anything by Christmas either, and decided that perhaps it wasn't meant to be.

"Finally at the end of January, the editor called and asked me to come by the office to have my picture taken for the column, which would start that next week. I was amazed, and couldn't wait to tell my group!

"As I looked back, I realized that I couldn't have started a weekly column any sooner, because the holiday season had been so hectic. Yes, God's timing *was* perfect.

"I thanked God, and I thanked my group for giving me the courage to make that first call, and for the continued, weekly challenge to define my dream in daily, manageable steps."

ESSENTIAL STEP #4

I have seen in my life, and in the lives of hundreds of friends and acquaintances who struggle with addiction, how an encounter with the living, loving God brings immediate relief from guilt, shame, and hopelessness. Yet, without the encouragement and support of an accountability group, very few people sustain lifestyle changes over any length of time.

For those who cannot depend on family or friends, or are unable to go through the initial withdrawals alone, an accountability group can bring daily, even hourly physical support to a person's moment-by-moment struggle to overcome certain addictions. It is also a place to be encouraged and cheered on for successfully making difficult lifestyle changes.

As you attempt to make difficult or positive changes, or achieve certain goals in your life, don't hesitate to ask others to keep you on track. As they ask you helpful questions, call you with timely reminders, and encourage you with notes and E-mails along the way, you will feel more motivated to reach your specific goal, develop a new habit, or eliminate an old habit.

Accountability will sustain you as you change your life one day at a time, one dream at a time!

NINE

The Four Essential Steps That Will Change Your Life!

The question is not "Do I need to change?" The question you and I must ask ourselves is "What or where do I need to change?"

Every person reading this book (for that matter, every person who is born and lives) has weaknesses and shortcomings. Each one of us has past experiences where we have been wounded or have wounded another. These irreversible life experiences have affected who we are, how we act, love, give, forgive, parent, nurture, and dream. This book is not about digging into your life to *come up* with areas that might need to change. This is a book that accepts and acknowledges that life is *all about* change.

I am absolutely convinced that awareness; admission; a daily, written action plan; and accountability *will change your life*—one day, one hour, one workout, one appointment with God at a time *beginning today.*

ESSENTIAL STEP #1: CHANGE BEGINS
WITH AWARENESS

Becoming whole, healed, and fulfilled men and women begins with the awareness that you and I are not perfect and will never be perfect. Identifying the areas where we are wounded, handicapped, out of control, hurt, in pain, wrong, or unfair is the first essential step to changing our lives for the better. Psychologists, clergy, and recovery experts refer to the identification process as examining yourself or "taking an inventory."

But if you *still* struggle with acknowledging your shortcomings, there is one more method for self-discovery. Make a list of what others do that irritates, angers, or bothers you. This list will give you a mirror of your own shortcomings. Those in the self-help field will tell you that this is called "projection."

Recently, I spoke to hundreds of people and made the comment that "I was not raised by a nurturing mother." Three days later, my twenty-year-old son fell snow-boarding and had to have outpatient knee surgery. I was in the last push of a writing deadline. So, guess who I called? My mother.

I asked her to come to my house for the weekend and be the "on-call" nurse to Jake. I knew he would need attention, food, a mother's love, and medicine. I also knew that she would drop everything to give loving care to her grandson. In fact, she drove over to my house that night, made homemade chicken soup *and* beef stew, took regular snacks upstairs to him, and did all the many dishes. Before she left in the morning for her 8 A.M. tee time, she left his pills out on the table with a note.

I got up right after she left and had my one-hour appointment with God. In the "thanks section," I proceeded to thank God for my "nurturing" mother. As I finished the sentence, my jaw dropped. My mother *is* nurturing. I am not.

Not one of us can point a finger at someone else without honestly examining our own lives and acknowledging that we've done the same thing or have possibly hurt another person in the same way. *Every* human being has prejudices, blind spots, shortcomings, wounded hearts and minds, and falls short of perfection.

The first essential step to change is to identify—become aware of—the areas where we are weak, wrong, unforgiving, or blind so that we might change our lives for the better, fulfill our dreams, and make a positive difference in the world. You can take the step of awareness today, right now.

ESSENTIAL STEP #2: CHANGE IS EMPOWERED BY ADMISSION

The second essential and most natural step toward changing our lives is to admit our individual areas of defect to ourselves, others, and God.

Outward or public admission of our problems, sins, shortcomings, or failures is both a recovery and biblical principle. It has been found by each of these areas of study to be the point where power to change is released.

The Twelve Steps are based on admitting your shortcomings to yourself, others, and to a higher power. The Twelve Steps encourage you to examine yourself, rather than blame others. It is a step-by-step approach to changing your life by methodically and deliberately admitting your shortcomings and making amends to others. The Twelve Steps encourage you to have an initial encounter with a higher power, where you ask for help to change, as well as spend time *daily* in meditation, asking for continued strength on the journey to change. Millions of people have been helped by the Twelve Steps.

The Judeo-Christian faith is also founded on biblical principles of forgiveness, truth, and confession. The Bible tells us that, through admission to others, we receive healing. With confession to God, we receive forgiveness, freedom, and cleansing from guilt and shame . . .

If my people, who are called by my name, will humble themselves and pray and seek my face and turn from their wicked ways, then will I hear from heaven and will forgive their sin and will heal their land.
II CHRONICLES 7:14

Humble yourself before the Lord and He will lift you up.
JAMES 4:10

The truth will set you free.
JOHN 8:32

Confess your sins to others so that you may be healed.
JAMES 5:16

If you confess your sins, He is faithful and just to forgive you your sins and cleanse you from all unrighteousness.
I JOHN 1:9

(All quotations from NIV.)

Confession that comes from a truthful and repentant heart that desires to turn from what is wrong is the action-step that releases God's supernatural power in your life to heal and change you physically, emotionally, spiritually, and mentally. I am convinced that my life irreversibly changed when I admitted I was wrong, had a real problem, and that I needed God's help to change. There is no other explanation that I can give for my changed desires, attitudes, convictions, and actions. I can point to a day and a place and a confession where I had an *encounter with God.* I met the living, loving God on August 26, 1976. I was forgiven and was healed and transformed by the all-powerful, all-knowing God of the Bible on that day. I didn't look to the sky and hope that something was up there to help me. I had an experience with the Father, Son, and Holy Spirit.

I am convinced that it was not a religion or a concept that had the power to change me. It was God's love toward me that touched my heart. It was both an intellectual and *emotional* understanding that He sent His Only Son to earth to die on a cross for me. His act of love motivated me to love Him. When I received forgiveness (that felt like a cleansing shower), I knew I didn't deserve it. I was forever changed by the knowledge that God loved me and gave me—and anyone who believes in Him and accepts the sacrifice of His Son in place of their sins—a fresh start on earth and a promise of a place in eternity forever.

My simple, life-changing story has remained the same for over two decades. I have witnesses from twenty-four years ago who can attest to my abruptly changed character and sobriety. My dramatically changed life is powerful proof that I was met and loved and changed by the living, loving God on August 26, 1976.

Though it has not always been easy, I have never looked back. I have been unashamedly compelled to tell others that "You will receive power to change if you will admit your sins to God and ask *all* of Him—Father, Son, and Holy Spirit—to come into *all* of you!"

I am convinced that when we are honest and truthful about

our lives in front of God and others, we will receive healing, forgiveness, encouragement, some rejection, some deserved consequences, and ultimately a new freedom to go on and fulfill our destiny!

You can take this admission-step today. Write a letter, pick up a phone, drive over to his or her house, step into his or her office, walk into his or her bedroom—and apologize. Share with the person whom you have hurt what you have done and that you are sorry. Ask him or her to forgive you.

You can take this step today with God. If you have never been introduced to the living, loving God, then let me be your "janitor." Express to Him in your own words where you have missed the mark or how you have fallen short. Then ask Him to forgive you. Acknowledge that He is the God of the Bible who sent His Son to earth two thousand years ago to die for your sins. Thank Him for such a sacrificial act of love. And tell Him that you love Him and want to know Him better.

With that prayer of admission, the life-changing power of the living, loving God will immediately begin to fill you and change your life—every aspect of it—for the better.

ESSENTIAL STEP #3: CHANGE IS ACHIEVED THROUGH A DAILY ACTION PLAN

The third essential step to achieve long-lasting change is to follow a daily, written action plan.

The secret to success is not a secret. Every successful person or company has achieved their goals or fulfilled their dreams by brainstorming, developing, and eventually designing a daily, written action plan. A written plan is essential to becoming and doing what you dream of. A written, daily action plan—that is followed step by step—is the process by which your goals will turn into reality.

Writing out—or listing—your goals, dreams, and plans and dividing them into tangible "to do's" will lead to success—if not 100% of the time, certainly more than if you don't write them out.

Do you want expert advice? Do you want unlimited power available to you? Do you want divine guidance and direction? Do you want to avoid impulsive mistakes? Do you want to know for what reason you were created? My suggestion is to take your written plan—the goals, ideas, hopes, and dreams—and share them in an appointment with the living, loving God every day.

For fifteen years, every day, I have found no better place to acquire valuable counsel than by having a written conversation with God where I both talk to Him and listen to Him. I simply pour my heart out to God in writing. My every aspiration, complaint, repentant thought, special request, and need is expressed on the lined pages of my journal. Though I can't see Him, I know that He hears me because He answers me.

I am just a sojourner on a path to live a fulfilling, exciting, purposeful life. I am not a theologian. And because religious philosophers and gurus abound, I live my life based on the premise that there can only be one truth and one God for all mankind. There is only one book that is called the Holy Bible. It is the Word of God. The Bible, consisting of the Old and New Testaments, is the unchanging, historical manuscript which reveals the person, character, love, and plan of God. Contained within every page is the voice of God for all generations.

Through the Bible, any person of any race has access to the words of the living, loving God. We never have to doubt, or guess, or search farther than the pages of a Bible if we want to hear God speak to us. He has given us letters, illustrations, principles, prayers, and commandments to live by. His voice is not magical or negotiable. It is the same for me as it is for my son. It was the same for my parents. It was the same for their parents. It will be the same for the generations to come. When I consider how to live my daily life, I consult with the Word of God to "get the plan!"

My two-way conversations with God have been the place where I have received the daily action plan for changing my life physically, emotionally, spiritually, and mentally. I am still learning to let go of what isn't good for me and to embrace what is best for me. I have had to become more patient than proactive. I have had to continually humble myself, make apologies, and fight off the lusts of my body and mind. And in the process, I believe I also have been able to make a difference in my world.

You can take this step today, as well. Gather a notebook or journal with plenty of blank paper (or **The change your life Daily Journal**), a pencil, and a Bible. If you don't have one or any of the above tools, go to the store today and get them.

Then, date the page and begin to journal. **The change your life Daily Journal** and **The change your life Daily Bible** provide a daily system for balancing your life physically, emotionally, spiritually, and mentally. The 8 Daily To Do's give you an opportunity to design a daily, written action plan that includes:

- Eating Right
- Exercising Regularly
- Forgiving
- Giving
- Talking to God
- Listening to God,
- Detailing Your Day, and
- Defining Your Dream.

Journaling is the practice where change is achieved by identifying and admitting to your struggles, as well as turning your goals, hopes, dreams, and To Do's into reality.

ESSENTIAL STEP #4: CHANGE IS SUSTAINED WITH ACCOUNTABILITY

I could not have changed so powerfully and positively, or so determinedly and passionately, without a family who embraced my effervescent faith, a husband who would keep me accountable to my sobriety, and a small group of friends who have supported and encouraged me in the tough times.

In order to sustain desired change in your life, accountability to a group is the fourth essential step to take. Whether you attend a Twelve Step group that is specific to your needs, a Bible study group (or a small group at your church) where you can learn to better integrate faith into every area of your life, or a **change your life Group** where you can be transparent and honest with friends with whom you've chosen to change, I encourage you to consider being accountable to a small group throughout your entire life.

This fourth and final step is a manageable, practical step that you can take *today!* Just call or ask at least two family members, coworkers, or friends to attend an existing group with you or to meet with you once a week for one hour for the next eight weeks.

Share the idea of how to keep a written record of your progress by journaling about all four areas of your life (physical, emotional, spiritual, and mental), even incorporating the 8 Daily To Do's into your daily journal experience. By your fourth meeting, decide if you need the additional support of a Twelve Step group in your area, and, if you do not currently attend a Bible teaching church, I would encourage you to make that your very next goal.

Each of the four essential steps to change requires that you make a choice. William James said, "When you have a choice to make and don't make it, that in itself is a choice." No matter how low you are, how far you have strayed, or how impossible or humiliating the changes ahead of you appear, allow my story to give you hope that the most broken of lives can achieve a healthy body, heal relationships, and connect with God. I urge you, if you have opened this book with even a faint willingness to change any area your life, to begin the process today.

I am living proof that the four essential steps to change—*awareness; admission; a daily, written action plan;* and *accountability*—will change your life . . .

one day,
one hour,
one workout,
one appointment with God
at a time.

The change
your life
Daily Journal

date _____

eat right

- understand your own body type, genetics, metabolism, etc.
- design a healthy, "plan ahead" eating plan that includes a balance of all the food groups in moderate portions
- **record your daily intentions for meals and snacks below**
- **review your progress and make daily adjustments**

breakfast _____

lunch _____

dinner _____

snacks _____

exercise regularly

- determine what type of activity, where, when, how often and with whom you most like to exercise
- develop a "week at a glance" exercise plan that includes a variety of 3 to 4 activities and has provision for alternate dates and times.

Detail your week plan; highlight today's plan.... what? when? where? with whom?

sun	mon	tue	wed	thur	fri	sat

journal

Journal below about any temptations, circumstances or emotions—today— that might keep you from reaching your goals? (ex: vacation, celebrations, etc.)

_____

_____

_____

_____

_____

_____

p
h
y
s
i
c
a
l

change
your
life
daily

date _____

e
m
o
t
i
o
n
a
l

forgive

To experience emotional balance on a daily basis, allow one or more of the below questions to prompt you to journal about the relationships in your life that need to heal and be healed.

Today, I know I need to ask _____ **to forgive me.**

I need to forgive myself for _____

I need to forgive _____ **for** _____

And I ask God to forgive me for _____

_____

_____

_____

_____

_____

_____

_____

What additional step(s) can I take to complete the healing that I have just journaled about in the above space? (ex: a phone call, letter, apology, etc.)

_____

_____

_____

_____

give

The gift of time, money, resources, or talent to an organization or person is both a powerful and practical way to help others.
What need comes to my mind—today—that I can find and fill and/or what person or organization needs a specific source of comfort or encouragement that I can give?

_____

_____

_____

_____

_____

change
your
life
daily

_____

date _____

talk to God

**Today, in honest transparency, share—in writing—your thoughts,
gratitude, regrets, fears, plans, hopes, dreams and requests
for yourself and others with the living, loving God.**

s
p
i
r
i
t
u
a
l

_____

_____

_____

_____

_____

_____

_____

_____

_____

_____

_____

_____

_____

_____

_____

listen to God

God's voice is found in His word, the Bible.
Unless you have another system, read today's **change your life** **Daily Bible**
using Today's Date. Write in this area, any verse or verses that stand out,
touch your heart, encourage or correct you. **What is God saying to you today?**

_____

_____

_____

_____

_____

_____

change
your
life
daily

date _____

m
e
n
t
a
l

detail your day

appointments

quiet time ☐
work out ☐
_____ ☐
_____ ☐
_____ ☐
_____ ☐
_____ ☐
_____ ☐
_____ ☐
_____ ☐
_____ ☐
_____ ☐
_____ ☐
_____ ☐
_____ ☐
_____ ☐
_____ ☐
_____ ☐

calls to make   *phone #*

_____
_____
_____
_____

letters to write/fax/email
                    w f e
_____ ☐ ☐ ☐
_____ ☐ ☐ ☐
_____ ☐ ☐ ☐
_____ ☐ ☐ ☐

things to do

_____ ☐
_____ ☐
_____ ☐
_____ ☐
_____ ☐

define your dream

What is one practical step you can take toward reaching a goal—
and fulfilling a dream—in one or more areas of your life?
Use this space to brainstorm or to develop a dream that won't go away!

physical | emotional
mental | spiritual

change
your
life
daily

date _____

eat right
- understand your own body type, genetics, metabolism, etc.
- design a healthy, "plan ahead" eating plan that includes a balance of all the food groups in moderate portions
- **record your daily intentions for meals and snacks below**
- **review your progress and make daily adjustments**

breakfast _____

lunch _____

dinner _____

snacks _____

exercise regularly
- determine what type of activity, where, when, how often and with whom you most like to exercise
- develop a "week at a glance" exercise plan that includes a variety of 3 to 4 activities and has provision for alternate dates and times.

Detail your week plan; highlight today's plan.... what? when? where? with whom?

sun	mon	tue	wed	thur	fri	sat

journal
Journal below about any temptations, circumstances or emotions—today—that might keep you from reaching your goals? (ex: vacation, celebrations, etc.)

_____

_____

_____

_____

_____

p
h
y
s
i
c
a
l

change
your
life
daily

date _____

e
m
o
t
i
o
n
a
l

forgive

To experience emotional balance on a daily basis, allow one or more of the below questions to prompt you to journal about the relationships in your life that need to heal and be healed.

Today, I know I need to ask _____ **to forgive me.**

I need to forgive myself for _____

I need to forgive _____ **for** _____

And I ask God to forgive me for _____

_____

_____

_____

_____

_____

_____

What additional step(s) can I take to complete the healing that I have just journaled about in the above space? (ex: a phone call, letter, apology, etc.)

_____

_____

_____

_____

give

The gift of time, money, resources, or talent to an organization or person is both a powerful and practical way to help others.
What need comes to my mind—today—that I can find and fill and/or what person or organization needs a specific source of comfort or encouragement that I can give?

_____

_____

_____

_____

_____

change
your
life
daily

date _____

talk to God

Today, in honest transparency, share—in writing—your thoughts, gratitude, regrets, fears, plans, hopes, dreams and requests for yourself and others with the living, loving God.

_____

_____

_____

_____

_____

_____

_____

_____

_____

_____

_____

_____

_____

_____

_____

_____

_____

_____

listen to God

God's voice is found in His word, the Bible.
Unless you have another system, read today's **change your life** Daily Bible using Today's Date. Write in this area, any verse or verses that stand out, touch your heart, encourage or correct you. **What is God saying to you today?**

_____

_____

_____

_____

_____

_____

s
p
i
r
i
t
u
a
l

change
your
life
daily

date _____

m
e
n
t
a
l

detail your day

appointments

	☐
quiet time	☐
work out	☐
	☐
	☐
	☐
	☐
	☐
	☐
	☐
	☐
	☐
	☐
	☐
	☐
	☐
	☐
	☐

calls to make *phone #*

_____
_____
_____
_____

letters to write/fax/email
              w f e
_____ ☐ ☐ ☐
_____ ☐ ☐ ☐
_____ ☐ ☐ ☐
_____ ☐ ☐ ☐

things to do

_____ ☐
_____ ☐
_____ ☐
_____ ☐
_____ ☐

define your dream

What is one practical step you can take toward reaching a goal—
and fulfilling a dream—in one or more areas of your life?
Use this space to brainstorm or to develop a dream that won't go away!

physical | emotional
mental | spiritual

change
your
life
daily

date _____

eat right
· understand your own body type, genetics, metabolism, etc.
· design a healthy, "plan ahead" eating plan that includes a balance
  of all the food groups in moderate portions
· **record your daily intentions for meals and snacks below**
· **review your progress and make daily adjustments**

breakfast _____

lunch _____

dinner _____

snacks _____

exercise regularly
· determine what type of activity, where, when, how often and with whom you
  most like to exercise
· develop a "week at a glance" exercise plan that includes a variety of 3 to 4 activities
  and has provision for alternate dates and times.

Detail your week plan; highlight today's plan.... what? when? where? with whom?

sun	mon	tue	wed	thur	fri	sat

journal
**Journal below about any temptations, circumstances or emotions—today—
that might keep you from reaching your goals?** (ex: vacation, celebrations, etc.)

_____

_____

_____

_____

_____

_____

p
h
y
s
i
c
a
l

change
your
life
daily

date _____

e
m
o
t
i
o
n
a
l

forgive

To experience emotional balance on a daily basis, allow one or more of the below questions to prompt you to journal about the relationships in your life that need to heal and be healed.

Today, I know I need to ask _____ **to forgive me.**

I need to forgive myself for _____

I need to forgive _____ **for** _____

And I ask God to forgive me for _____

_____

_____

_____

_____

_____

_____

_____

What additional step(s) can I take to complete the healing that I have just journaled about in the above space? (ex: a phone call, letter, apology, etc.)

_____

_____

_____

_____

give

The gift of time, money, resources, or talent to an organization or person is both a powerful and practical way to help others.
What need comes to my mind—today—that I can find and fill and/or what person or organization needs a specific source of comfort or encouragement that I can give?

_____

_____

_____

_____

_____

_____

change
your
life
daily

date _____

talk to God

Today, in honest transparency, share—in writing—your thoughts,
gratitude, regrets, fears, plans, hopes, dreams and requests
for yourself and others with the living, loving God.

_____
_____
_____
_____
_____
_____
_____
_____
_____
_____
_____
_____
_____
_____
_____
_____
_____
_____

s
p
i
r
i
t
u
a
l

listen to God

God's voice is found in His word, the Bible.
Unless you have another system, read today's **change your life** Daily Bible
using Today's Date. Write in this area, any verse or verses that stand out,
touch your heart, encourage or correct you. **What is God saying to you today?**

_____
_____
_____
_____
_____
_____

change
your
life
daily

date _____

m
e
n
t
a
l

detail your day

appointments

quiet time	☐
work out	☐
	☐
	☐
	☐
	☐
	☐
	☐
	☐
	☐
	☐
	☐
	☐
	☐
	☐
	☐
	☐

calls to make   *phone #*

_____

_____

_____

_____

_____

letters to write/fax/email
w   f   e
☐ ☐ ☐

☐ ☐ ☐

☐ ☐ ☐

☐ ☐ ☐

things to do

_____ ☐

_____ ☐

_____ ☐

_____ ☐

_____ ☐

define your dream

What is one practical step you can take toward reaching a goal—
and fulfilling a dream—in one or more areas of your life?
Use this space to brainstorm or to develop a dream that won't go away!

physical	emotional
mental	spiritual

change
your
life
daily

date _____

eat right

- · understand your own body type, genetics, metabolism, etc.
- · design a healthy, "plan ahead" eating plan that includes a balance of all the food groups in moderate portions
- · **record your daily intentions for meals and snacks below**
- · **review your progress and make daily adjustments**

breakfast
_____
_____
lunch
_____
_____
dinner
_____
_____
snacks
_____

exercise regularly

- · determine what type of activity, where, when, how often and with whom you most like to exercise
- · develop a "week at a glance" exercise plan that includes a variety of 3 to 4 activities and has provision for alternate dates and times.

Detail your week plan; highlight today's plan.... what? when? where? with whom?

sun	mon	tue	wed	thur	fri	sat

journal

Journal below about any temptations, circumstances or emotions—today— that might keep you from reaching your goals? (ex: vacation, celebrations, etc.)

_____
_____
_____
_____
_____
_____

p
h
y
s
i
c
a
l

change
your
life
daily

date_____

e
m
o
t
i
o
n
a
l

forgive

To experience emotional balance on a daily basis, allow one or more of the below questions to prompt you to journal about the relationships in your life that need to heal and be healed.

Today, I know I need to ask _____ **to forgive me.**

I need to forgive myself for _____

I need to forgive _____ **for** _____

And I ask God to forgive me for _____

_____

_____

_____

_____

_____

_____

_____

What additional step(s) can I take to complete the healing that I have just journaled about in the above space? (ex: a phone call, letter, apology, etc.)

_____

_____

_____

_____

give

The gift of time, money, resources, or talent to an organization or person is both a powerful and practical way to help others.
What need comes to my mind—today—that I can find and fill and/or what person or organization needs a specific source of comfort or encouragement that I can give?

_____

_____

_____

_____

_____

_____

change
your
life
daily

date _____

talk to God

Today, in honest transparency, share—in writing—your thoughts, gratitude, regrets, fears, plans, hopes, dreams and requests for yourself and others with the living, loving God.

_____
_____
_____
_____
_____
_____
_____
_____
_____
_____
_____
_____
_____
_____
_____
_____
_____

s
p
i
r
i
t
u
a
l

listen to God

God's voice is found in His word, the Bible.
Unless you have another system, read today's **change your life Daily Bible**
using Today's Date. Write in this area, any verse or verses that stand out,
touch your heart, encourage or correct you. **What is God saying to you today?**

_____
_____
_____
_____
_____
_____

change
your
life
daily

date _____

m   **detail your day**
e
n   **appointments** ☐   **calls to make**   *phone #*
t   *quiet time* ☐   _____
a   *work out* ☐   _____
l   _____ ☐   _____

appointments		calls to make phone #
quiet time	☐	_____
work out	☐	_____
_____	☐	_____
_____	☐	
_____	☐	**letters to write/fax/email**
_____	☐	*w f e*
_____	☐	_____ ☐ ☐ ☐
_____	☐	_____ ☐ ☐ ☐
_____	☐	_____ ☐ ☐ ☐
_____	☐	_____ ☐ ☐ ☐
_____	☐	**things to do**
_____	☐	_____ ☐
_____	☐	_____ ☐
_____	☐	_____ ☐
_____	☐	_____ ☐
_____	☐	_____ ☐

define your dream

What is one practical step you can take toward reaching a goal—
and fulfilling a dream—in one or more areas of your life?
Use this space to brainstorm or to develop a dream that won't go away!

physical	emotional
mental	spiritual

change
your
life
daily

date _____

eat right

- understand your own body type, genetics, metabolism, etc.
- design a healthy, "plan ahead" eating plan that includes a balance of all the food groups in moderate portions
- **record your daily intentions for meals and snacks below**
- **review your progress and make daily adjustments**

breakfast _____

lunch _____

dinner _____

snacks _____

exercise regularly

- determine what type of activity, where, when, how often and with whom you most like to exercise
- develop a "week at a glance" exercise plan that includes a variety of 3 to 4 activities and has provision for alternate dates and times.

Detail your week plan; highlight today's plan.... what? when? where? with whom?

sun	mon	tue	wed	thur	fri	sat

journal

**Journal below about any temptations, circumstances or emotions—today—
that might keep you from reaching your goals?** (ex: vacation, celebrations, etc.)

_____

_____

_____

_____

_____

_____

p
h
y
s
i
c
a
l

change
your
life
daily

date _____

e
m
o
t
i
o
n
a
l

forgive

To experience emotional balance on a daily basis, allow one or more of the below questions to prompt you to journal about the relationships in your life that need to heal and be healed.

Today, I know I need to ask _____ **to forgive me.**

I need to forgive myself for _____

I need to forgive _____ **for** _____

And I ask God to forgive me for _____

_____

_____

_____

_____

_____

_____

_____

What additional step(s) can I take to complete the healing that I have just journaled about in the above space? (ex: a phone call, letter, apology, etc.)

_____

_____

_____

give

The gift of time, money, resources, or talent to an organization or person is both a powerful and practical way to help others.
What need comes to my mind—today—that I can find and fill and/or what person or organization needs a specific source of comfort or encouragement that I can give?

_____

_____

_____

_____

_____

_____

change
your
life
daily

date _____

talk to God

Today, in honest transparency, share—in writing—your thoughts, gratitude, regrets, fears, plans, hopes, dreams and requests for yourself and others with the living, loving God.

s
p
i
r
i
t
u
a
l

_____
_____
_____
_____
_____
_____
_____
_____
_____
_____
_____
_____
_____
_____
_____
_____
_____
_____

listen to God

God's voice is found in His word, the Bible.
Unless you have another system, read today's **change your life** Daily Bible using Today's Date. Write in this area, any verse or verses that stand out, touch your heart, encourage or correct you. **What is God saying to you today?**

_____
_____
_____
_____
_____
_____
_____

change
your
life
daily

date _____

m
e
n
t
a
l

detail your day

appointments

- *quiet time* ☐
- *work out* ☐
- ☐
- ☐
- ☐
- ☐
- ☐
- ☐
- ☐
- ☐
- ☐
- ☐
- ☐
- ☐
- ☐
- ☐

calls to make   *phone #*

_____

_____

_____

_____

letters to write/fax/email
            w f e
_____ ☐ ☐ ☐

_____ ☐ ☐ ☐

_____ ☐ ☐ ☐

_____ ☐ ☐ ☐

things to do

_____ ☐

_____ ☐

_____ ☐

_____ ☐

_____ ☐

define your dream

What is one practical step you can take toward reaching a goal—
and fulfilling a dream—in one or more areas of your life?
Use this space to brainstorm or to develop a dream that won't go away!

physical	emotional
mental	spiritual

change
your
life
daily

date _____

eat right

- · understand your own body type, genetics, metabolism, etc.
- · design a healthy, "plan ahead" eating plan that includes a balance of all the food groups in moderate portions
- · **record your daily intentions for meals and snacks below**
- · **review your progress and make daily adjustments**

breakfast _____

lunch _____

dinner _____

snacks _____

exercise regularly

- · determine what type of activity, where, when, how often and with whom you most like to exercise
- · develop a "week at a glance" exercise plan that includes a variety of 3 to 4 activities and has provision for alternate dates and times.

Detail your week plan; highlight today's plan.... what? when? where? with whom?

sun	mon	tue	wed	thur	fri	sat

journal

Journal below about any temptations, circumstances or emotions—today—that might keep you from reaching your goals? (ex: vacation, celebrations, etc.)

_____

_____

_____

_____

_____

_____

p
h
y
s
i
c
a
l

change
your
life
daily

date _____

emotional

forgive

To experience emotional balance on a daily basis, allow one or more of the below questions to prompt you to journal about the relationships in your life that need to heal and be healed.

Today, I know I need to ask _____ **to forgive me.**

I need to forgive myself for _____

I need to forgive _____ **for** _____

And I ask God to forgive me for _____

_____

_____

_____

_____

_____

_____

_____

What additional step(s) can I take to complete the healing that I have just journaled about in the above space? (ex: a phone call, letter, apology, etc.)

_____

_____

_____

give

The gift of time, money, resources, or talent to an organization or person is both a powerful and practical way to help others.
What need comes to my mind—today—that I can find and fill and/or what person or organization needs a specific source of comfort or encouragement that I can give?

_____

_____

_____

_____

_____

_____

change
your
life
daily

date _____

talk to God

**Today, in honest transparency, share—in writing—your thoughts,
gratitude, regrets, fears, plans, hopes, dreams and requests
for yourself and others with the living, loving God.**

_____
_____
_____
_____
_____
_____
_____
_____
_____
_____
_____
_____
_____
_____
_____
_____

s
p
i
r
i
t
u
a
l

listen to God

God's voice is found in His word, the Bible.
Unless you have another system, read today's **change your life** Daily Bible
using Today's Date. Write in this area, any verse or verses that stand out,
touch your heart, encourage or correct you. **What is God saying to you today?**

_____
_____
_____
_____
_____
_____

change
your
life
daily

date _____

m
e
n
t
a
l

detail your day

appointments

quiet time ☐
work out ☐
☐
☐
☐
☐
☐
☐
☐
☐
☐
☐
☐
☐
☐
☐
☐

calls to make   *phone #*

_____
_____
_____
_____
_____

letters to write/fax/email
w f e
_____ ☐ ☐ ☐
_____ ☐ ☐ ☐
_____ ☐ ☐ ☐
_____ ☐ ☐ ☐

things to do

_____ ☐
_____ ☐
_____ ☐
_____ ☐
_____ ☐

define your dream

What is one practical step you can take toward reaching a goal—
and fulfilling a dream—in one or more areas of your life?
Use this space to brainstorm or to develop a dream that won't go away!

physical | emotional
mental | spiritual

change
your
life
daily

date _____

eat right

- · understand your own body type, genetics, metabolism, etc.
- · design a healthy, "plan ahead" eating plan that includes a balance of all the food groups in moderate portions
- · **record your daily intentions for meals and snacks below**
- · **review your progress and make daily adjustments**

breakfast	
lunch	
dinner	
snacks	

exercise regularly

- · determine what type of activity, where, when, how often and with whom you most like to exercise
- · develop a "week at a glance" exercise plan that includes a variety of 3 to 4 activities and has provision for alternate dates and times.

Detail your week plan; highlight today's plan.... what? when? where? with whom?

sun	mon	tue	wed	thur	fri	sat

journal

Journal below about any temptations, circumstances or emotions—today—that might keep you from reaching your goals? (ex: vacation, celebrations, etc.)

_____

_____

_____

_____

_____

_____

p
h
y
s
i
c
a
l

change
your
life
daily

date _____

forgive

To experience emotional balance on a daily basis, allow one or more of the below questions to prompt you to journal about the relationships in your life that need to heal and be healed.

Today, I know I need to ask _____ **to forgive me.**

I need to forgive myself for _____

I need to forgive _____ **for** _____

And I ask God to forgive me for _____

_____

_____

_____

_____

_____

_____

What additional step(s) can I take to complete the healing that I have just journaled about in the above space? (ex: a phone call, letter, apology, etc.)

_____

_____

_____

_____

give

The gift of time, money, resources, or talent to an organization or person is both a powerful and practical way to help others.
What need comes to my mind—today—that I can find and fill and/or what person or organization needs a specific source of comfort or encouragement that I can give?

_____

_____

_____

_____

_____

_____

date _____

talk to God

Today, in honest transparency, share—in writing—your thoughts, gratitude, regrets, fears, plans, hopes, dreams and requests for yourself and others with the living, loving God.

_____
_____
_____
_____
_____
_____
_____
_____
_____
_____
_____
_____
_____
_____
_____
_____
_____
_____

s
p
i
r
i
t
u
a
l

listen to God

God's voice is found in His word, the Bible.
Unless you have another system, read today's **change your life Daily Bible** using Today's Date. Write in this area, any verse or verses that stand out, touch your heart, encourage or correct you. **What is God saying to you today?**

_____
_____
_____
_____
_____
_____
_____

change
your
life
daily

date _____

m
e   ### detail your day
n
t   #### appointments   **calls to make**   *phone #*
a
l   *quiet time* ☐   _____

         work out ☐   _____

         _____ ☐   _____

         _____ ☐   _____

         _____ ☐   _____

         _____ ☐   _____

         _____ ☐   **letters to write/fax/email**
                                              w   f   e
         _____ ☐   ☐ ☐ ☐
         _____ ☐   _____ ☐ ☐ ☐
         _____ ☐   _____ ☐ ☐ ☐
         _____ ☐   _____ ☐ ☐ ☐
         _____ ☐   _____ ☐ ☐ ☐

         _____ ☐   **things to do**

         _____ ☐   _____ ☐

         _____ ☐   _____ ☐

         _____ ☐   _____ ☐

         _____ ☐   _____ ☐

         _____ ☐   _____ ☐

define your dream

What is one practical step you can take toward reaching a goal—
and fulfilling a dream—in one or more areas of your life?
Use this space to brainstorm or to develop a dream that won't go away!

| physical | emotional |
| mental | spiritual |

change
your
life
daily

The change your life Group Leader's Guide

Before the 1ST Meeting

LEADER PREPARATION

Make sure that each member of the group has **The change your life Journal** and **The change your life Bible** or a compatible Bible and journal at least two weeks before the first meeting.

Send out reminder postcards one week before the meeting, and even make a reminder phone call the day or night before you meet for the first time.

Become familiar with each of the four *daily* pages (**Physical, Emotional, Spiritual,** and **Mental**) and the 8 Daily To Do's.

Prepare a sheet of paper for all members to write down their names, addresses, and phone numbers.

Think of an interesting comment for everyone to share when they introduce themselves, such as:

- How many children do you have, or would you like to have?
- When is your birthday?
- Describe yourself in one word.

Make sure you have a watch or alarm clock and a pad of paper and pen for notes.

Meeting One

1. Have name tags.
2. Listen to a selected portion of **The change your life Motivational Audio** as a group. (Optional. See end of book for ordering information.)
3. Explain each of the four balanced life pages in **The change your life Daily Journal** (**Physical, Emotional, Spiritual,** and **Mental**), so that everyone understands the format. Be sure that no one feels uncertain on how to journal.
4. Make sure everyone knows how to read through **The change your life Daily Bible.** There may be members who have never read a Bible. Explain how to look up each day's reading by looking up today's date. If a member is unfamiliar with the Bible or has limited time, you might encourage them to read only the New Testament, Proverbs, and Psalms this year, then add the Old Testament reading to their routine next year. Be sure to emphasize that Bible reading is an integral part of the daily journaling experience, as you are all reading the same chapters and verses on the same days.
5. Briefly discuss your personal expectations and desires to change. Depending on how much time you have, ask a few people to share one or two of their struggles.
6. Exchange phone numbers, so that each member of the group gets a "remember to journal" reminder call in the morning.

ASSIGNMENT

Journal for the week—all four balanced life pages—every day! If you are using **The change your life Daily Journal,** fill in the two-month calendar to make it current. Mark on the calendar what time you plan to journal each day.

Meeting Two

LEADER PREPARATION

Type or hand-write the names, addresses, and phone numbers of each member of the group. Make enough copies for each person in the group.

Assess your own success this week. Did you enjoy doing the **Daily Journal?** What area, if any, did you struggle to get through? Did you notice one area of your life that needs more balance than another? Be ready to discuss some of your own experiences this week.

THE MEETING

1. Welcome any newcomers to the group who might have missed the first meeting. (After the first week, encourage new members to wait for the next eight-week session or to begin their own **change your life Group.** A group finds the sharing time more confidential and comfortable if the group members remain constant.)

2. Pass out the list of phone numbers and addresses. This list can be used as a phone chain where each person calls the

name immediately listed below their name. This will allow the group to begin to hold itself accountable to meet on time, complete weekly assignments, and update each other on last-minute adjustments to the schedule.

3. When you ask group questions, make sure that you state the question clearly. Ask who would like to begin or suggest, "Would the person who's the oldest (youngest) like to start?" If the group is timid, you might briefly give your answer as an example, then suggest that you move to the person on your left.

Questions for Group Discussion:

1. Which section of the journal seemed the most helpful/insightful? Which section was the hardest to work through?
2. Is there a specific area (Physical, Emotional, Spiritual, or Mental) of your life that is particularly out of balance or that you would like to change? Explain.

ASSIGNMENT

Journal for the week—all four pages daily! Choose a person in your **change your life Group** to be your accountability partner. Ask them to keep you accountable to something specific, such as three workouts per week, controlling your temper with your children, or calling you each day to remind you to have your journal appointment.

Meeting Three

LEADER PREPARATION

From this week's journal pages, choose a victory or defeat in each of your 8 Daily To Do's (**Eat Right, Exercise Regularly, Forgive, Give, Talk to God, Listen to God, Detail Your Day,** and **Define Your Dream**). Ask the group members to share, but be prepared to go first and give an example. Be brief but vulnerable!

THE MEETING

Questions for Group Discussion:

1. What hinders you from being honest with others about your struggles? (Examples: Fear of failure? Having to admit a weakness? Appearing weak? Being rejected or less respected or liked?)

2. If the group is *less* than five people, go through *each* section of the 8 Daily To Do's (**Eat Right, Exercise Regularly, Forgive, Give, Talk to God, Listen to God, Detail Your Day,** and **Define Your Dream**). Discuss a defeat and a victory (or what is called "a pit and a peak"). If the group is *more* than five people, have everyone share one victory and one defeat from each of the four journal pages/areas (Physical, Emotional, Spiritual, and Mental).

3. Share any unexpected emotions or issues that occurred during your journal experience this week.

End today's meeting with the accountability partners (from last week) praying for each other. (This can be short, silent, or out loud. Let each pair decide how they want to pray for each other.)

ASSIGNMENT

Journal for the week—all four balanced life pages—every day! Set one to two thirty-day and longer-term (six months or a year) goals for each page: Physical, Emotional, Spiritual, and Mental. These goals can range from a general, e.g.: "I'd like to be a more giving person," to the very specific, "I want to work out four times a week for one hour each time over the next thirty days."

Meeting Four

LEADER PREPARATION

Write your goals out on three-by-five cards or place them strategically in your **Daily Journal** as a daily, visual motivator. Be prepared to show the group your example.

THE MEETING

1. Rate yourself on a scale from one to ten in each of the four balanced life pages from the previous week. Share how successful you were in your commitment to journal every day.
2. Share one (or more) of your thirty-day goals and one long-term aspiration. (Each person will determine how many of their goals they will share based on their total allotted

time. If they are fast talkers, and to the point, they will share more goals. The more analytical or melancholy person will usually reflect on only one goal during her allotted time.)

3. Is there something that you have always dreamed of doing but were afraid to do? Why?

4. Would you be willing to brainstorm how to turn that dream into a reality? (If there is time, open up the group for a one-minute per person brainstorm session.)

End the meeting with the accountability partners praying for each other.

ASSIGNMENT

Journal for the week—all four balanced life pages—every day! Write out your goals in a place that will serve as a visual reminder to you this week. In the **Detail Your Day** and **Define Your Dream** sections of **The change your life Daily Journal,** as well as on the Calendar page, schedule specific times and ways to achieve these goals.

Meeting Five

LEADER PREPARATION

Send a personal card or note to each person in the group this week. Be sure to encourage them to pursue the specific changes they would like to make or to reach the goals that they have set.

THE MEETING

By now, most members of your group have been able to pinpoint one or more areas of their lives that need more balance or change. Be sure to emphasize that the group meeting is important to keep each person motivated on a weekly basis. Discuss the importance of the daily habit of journaling. Acknowledge that it is a difficult but rewarding habit that develops over time with discipline and consistency.

Questions for Group Discussion:

1. What time of day do you find that journaling works best for you? Are you a morning person? A night person? Explain briefly.
2. Identify one of the long-term goals you discussed last week. Name the first step you will take toward fulfilling this goal. For example, if you desire to write a weekly article in a newspaper, what is the first step you will take? Will you write a letter to a local newspaper or make a phone call to a specific editor? Would you be willing to take any specific steps by next week?
3. Would you like to be held accountable to anyone in the group for those steps?

End today's meeting with the accountability partners praying for each other.

ASSIGNMENT

Journal for the week—all four pages daily! Focus on the **Listen to God** section. Underline or highlight at least one verse from the

Bible that has special meaning to you. Write that verse in the **Listen to God** section of your journal.

Meeting Six

LEADER PREPARATION

Be prepared to think about future options for either continuing the group or splitting off into two or three different **change your life Groups** with new members. (Spend no more than five minutes discussing your options *at the end* of the meeting. Set the alarm to go off early to allot time for this discussion.)

Remember to divide sharing time equally between each person—according to the number of people present each week. Once again, let the group know that you do this so that feelings are not hurt when you have to give them a thirty-second countdown. Remind them that this is a courtesy to allow everyone an opportunity to share. Always be sensitive to those who need a little extra time for sharing more deeply. As the leader, if you are the last person to share, you can always give up a little of your time to make up for any time losses.

THE MEETING

Questions for Group Discussion:

1. Rate yourself (one to ten) on how well you are doing in the **Listen to God** section on the **Spiritual** page. Briefly explain the "why" behind your rating.
2. Share one of the verses from the **Listen to God** section that held special meaning to you this week. (The leader

can go first in this case to give everyone an example of a verse that had particular meaning. If someone has not connected with God yet, ask them to share a verse they read that gave them comfort or one they simply liked.)

End today's meeting with the accountability partners praying for each other.

ASSIGNMENT

Journal for the week—all four pages daily! Focus on the **Forgive** and **Give** sections this week. Be prepared to share your journal experiences from the **Emotional** page.

Meeting Seven

LEADER PREPARATION

Have order forms ready in case the group wants to continue for another eight weeks and will need additional **Daily Journals.** (Our group went from September to May, with two- and three-week breaks for holidays. At each juncture, we added and subtracted members.)

If you have had a positive experience, consider others who might benefit from a **change your life Group** and give them a call. If the group seems as if it will be too big, plan to split off into a few groups with new leaders. Discuss how you can expand and reach out! (Limit this discussion time to five minutes at the end of the hour.)

THE MEETING

Questions for Group Discussion:

1. Explain your journal experience in the **Forgive** and **Give** sections during the past week. Rate yourself in both areas.
2. What patterns continue to plague your personality and undermine your personal success and growth? What section of the **Journal** does this appear in most frequently?
3. Think about the many relationships in your life. Is there someone who you are struggling to forgive? Share the situation with the group. Discuss how you will work through your forgiveness of them in a practical way. An amends letter? A phone call? An apology? A prayer?

End today's meeting with the accountability partners praying for each other.

ASSIGNMENT

Journal for the week—all four pages daily! If you have had trouble forgiving someone, write an apology letter to them this week, even if you are not going to mail it. Would you be willing to be held accountable—by the group—to make amends to that person?

Meeting Eight

LEADER PREPARATION

Look back over your notes from previous weeks—specifically at the positive changes, achieved goals, and improvements people have made. Take time to write a note that will encourage them to persevere in a certain area. Has it been discussed if the group is splitting off, continuing to meet, or taking a break? If not, do so.

THE MEETING

Questions for Group Discussion:

1. Rate your week—as a whole—on a scale from one to ten. Explain briefly.
2. Share about an apology letter you have written or read a specific journal entry from your **Forgive** section.
3. Share something encouraging about your accountability partner. For example, remind the group what he or she achieved, or a positive way in which change has been expressed in their life. (If someone's partner is not present, use your notes and share an encouraging, positive change about the person who is present.)
4. In what area have you seen the most change in your life? In what area do you desire to fulfill further goals, overcome specific weaknesses, and thus balance your life?
5. Share your greatest accomplishment or goal achieved over the past eight weeks.
6. How do you plan to sustain the changes you have made?

End today's meeting with the accountability partners praying for each other.

ASSIGNMENT

By now your group has developed a personality of its own. If you have decided to continue with your group, the camaraderie and openness you've shared will carry you through the weeks ahead. If you have decided to split up, encourage members to continue to journal and read the Bible daily, and always to persevere.

Product Order Form

___The CHANGE YOUR LIFE Daily Bible (365-day Bible) . . . $18

___The CHANGE YOUR LIFE Daily Journal (60-day Journal) . . . $17

___The CHANGE YOUR LIFE Walking Audio (2-part) series . . . $25

___Add 7.75% tax in California

___Shipping $2.50 per book

___Handling $2.00 per order

_____

$ Total

Include name, address, city, state, zip, and phone number. Send Visa, Master-Card, or Discover card number with expiration date, or make check payable to: **Becky Tirabassi, CHANGE YOUR LIFE, INC.**

For more information on Becky's CHANGE YOUR LIFE events, radio show, other motivational books, and resources, contact:

Becky Tirabassi, CHANGE YOUR LIFE, INC.
Box 9672
Newport Beach, CA 92660
or call 1-800-444-6189
or log on to **www.changeyourlifedaily.com**